The Divinity Doctrine

STEVEN BINKO

The Divinity Doctrine : A Metaphysical Guide
Copyright © 2014 Steven Binko

New Age, Metaphysics, Spirituality, Psychic Phenomena,
Religion, Life Improvement, Handbook

All rights reserved. No part of this book may be used or reproduced by any means, graphic, electronic, or mechanical, including photocopying, recording, taping or by any information storage retrieval system without the written permission of the author or publisher except in the case of brief quotations embodied in critical articles and reviews.

Cover Design & Author Photo edited by Wesley Souza

Illustrations by Steven Binko

Author Photo by Vicki Palombo, Photographic Memories/Palombo-Elliott

ISBN: 0615963617
ISBN-13: 978-0615963617

The views expressed in this work are solely those of the author and do not necessarily reflect the views of the publisher, and the publisher hereby disclaims any responsibility for them

The author of this book does not dispense medical advice or prescribe the use of any technique as a form of treatment for physical, emotional, or medical problems without the advice or a physician, either directly or indirectly. The intent of the author is only to offer insightful material on the subject matter covered. If the reader requires personal assistance or advice, a competent professional should be contacted.

The author, publisher and book producer specifically disclaim any responsibility for any liability, loss, or risk, personal or otherwise, which is incurred as a consequence, directly or indirectly, of the use and application of any of the contents of this book.

CHAPTER OVERVIEW

1	Angels & Guides	Pg 4
2	Animal Symbology	Pg 10
3	Ascension	Pg 24
4	Astral Projection	Pg 34
5	Astrology	Pg 42
6	Auras	Pg 58
7	Birthstones	Pg 62
8	Candles	Pg 66
9	Chakras	Pg 72
10	Crystals & Stones	Pg 78
11	Dowsing	Pg 96
12	Essential Oils	Pg 100
13	Grounding	Pg 106
14	Law of Attraction	Pg 112
15	Life Contracts	Pg 118
16	Ouija Boards	Pg 122
17	Psychics	Pg 126
18	Smudging	Pg 134
19	Tarot	Pg 138

Message from the Author

I remember years ago when I was just beginning to explore my gifts. Whenever I'd get out of school, my mom would drop me off at the bookstore to study. Instead, you'd find me sitting in the aisles with a pile of books about Psychics and Ghosts. Initially, I was overwhelmed by the mass amount of information. There were so many areas I was interested in, but I had no idea where to start. The one thing I kept looking for (but never found) was a "bible" about it all.

It was through this frustration and my years of experience that I decided to compose this book. Even as an experienced psychic-medium, I often find myself looking things up online or calling a mentor with questions. While I do believe that searching for understanding is part of the spiritual journey, I also know how helpful it would have been to have a handbook to guide me in my quest for understanding.

The title of this book, *The Divinity Doctrine*, was inspired a few years ago in a meditation session. I recall asking my guides to show me what my life purpose was. Each time I'd ask this question, I was shown what looked like a bible. As the leather binding opened, I could vaguely make out calligraphy and drawings on parchment pages. Stepping closer, the pictures transformed into a bright yellow light that prevented me from reading its contents. Asking what the book was about, I was told that the world needed a guide to life that was more applicable to these changing times. Wondering why I couldn't read it, I was told I had yet to write it! From that day forward, I knew that when the time was right, I would transform and illuminate the world with messages from beyond.

I can't sit here and tell you that I know everything about life, but I have so much that I felt obligated to share. Writing the last page of this book, I know that even after it reaches your hands, I'll continue to reflect on what else I would have liked to say. There were many areas I was interested in discussing but was guided to address at a later time. Furthermore, some of the topics I wanted to include (like Dream Analysis, Wicca and Numerology) are so expansive that they require a book of their own. Perhaps I will release additional volumes in the future. I genuinely hope, however, that of what I did include, something will connect with you on a soul level.

My experience writing these chapters was quite humorous. Pages that take two minutes for you to read often took me hours to write. Part of this is due to my being a perfectionist, but mostly because I had a hard time finding the vocabulary to adequately express my thoughts. The best way I can describe this is a near death experience (NDE). A lot of the time, people who've seen the other side and come back have a difficult time explaining colors for example. The reason for this is that outside of our dimension there are colors we can't begin to imagine, and which we don't have words for here on earth. Like this example, much of what I'm shown comes with a sense of knowing that's difficult for me to explain. I've tried to simplify everything to the best of my ability, but you can imagine how frustrating it is feeling mute when you have songs you'd like to scream from the mountain tops.

In spite of my religious upbringing, it's important for me to express my intentions with this material in depth. I never understood the debate between religion and spirituality. The truth is that both of these things share one thing in common: faith. While for some people these are two completely different concepts, it has been my experience that they're both partially integrated within each other. To be religious you must be spiritual as it involves faith in a creator, angels and figures not in the physical world. To be spiritual, it's not uncommon to have faith in a higher power or God, which is the foundation for many world religions. Nevertheless, to simply have faith is essential to grow on both our human and soul journeys. As someone who was raised with a religious background, but who lives in a spiritual lifestyle, it's impossible for me to say which way is right, as both have played such crucial roles in my life. It is this balance however, that I believe has helped me to understand people across the world.

If there is something that you connect with personally, I believe that you should follow it because it's authentic to you. It is the intention to connect with a higher source that is recognized, not the way which we go about doing so. More importantly, it's the way which we choose to live our lives. To simply attend church or be spiritual does not make you faithful, honest or selfless. Throughout the readings I've conducted, I've been reassured by my guides that your spiritual destination is not dependent on whether you live a life of religious faith or spirituality. It is your intentions and the way that you conduct your time on earth that is of the utmost importance.

When it comes to naming our Creator, you will notice I occasionally switch between the terms God, Spirit or Source. Personally, I connect with the term God most often, though for people who are not religious the connotations with this term may leave a disconnect. Understand that if I use the term God, this is not specific to a religious being. Considering the number of religions and spiritual ideas, I do not believe in a hierarchy of almighty figures leading us. I believe in a universal love and energy which we all answer to. As humans, we have simply adapted different names across the globe that often reflect connections to demographic, culture, upbringing and history.

I once spoke with a woman about Christianity who supported her faith with the fact that Christians are one of the largest religious populations in the world. Looking back a century ago, slavery was accepted as the social norm simply because Caucasians saw themselves as a dominant race in the United States. Just because something is widespread, however, does not make it right. This is not to say that Christianity is right or wrong, but simply to reiterate the fact that we need to respect people regardless of their religious and spiritual values – even if they fall into the minority. At the end of the day, we are all humans and the path we take to define our lives must remain authentic to our beliefs. It's our own choices we answer for in the end.

That being said, I ask you read this book with an open mind. Use it as a "general guide" for your metaphysical questions. Release the pressures to define where your beliefs lie. Instead, see what you connect with and consider true to yourself. It doesn't matter what your religious or spiritual views are – it's about your effort to examine, understand, and appreciate the life you were gifted, while constantly looking to improve it for yourself and others. Remember the value of unconditional, universal love, and you can never go wrong.

Last, but not least, thank you for picking up a copy of my guide. I'm so proud of it, and it's an honor to be part of your spiritual journey.

- Steven Binko

Chapter One

Guiding, protecting and serving between
the dimensions of heaven and earth.

ANGELS & GUIDES

On earth we have two spiritual forces that assist us in our daily lives – Angels and Guides. Though unseen by many, most of us have actually experienced their presence at one point or another. It's important to note that no matter your walk of life, Angels & Guides are readily able to help at your request. All you have to do is ask!

Angels

Of the three major world religions (Christianity, Judaism and Islam), all depict angels in their teachings. Beyond those religions, virtually all major walks of faith include some kind of celestial beings. Even before structured religion, depictions of "angel types" were seen in Egyptian and Greek culture. While opinions on angel classifications and purpose vary, it's clear there is a variety of heavenly beings that bridge the gap between the physical and spiritual worlds.

The angels that you're likely familiar with are the ones closest to our dimension; they deal specifically with our human experience. It's important to note that while their purpose is to initially provide protection, many angels end up providing guidance instead as our consciousness evolves.

Aside from the angels that guide us in our day-to-day lives, there are also beings known as archangels. The four you are likely familiar with are Gabriel, Michael, Raphael, and Uriel. Here are some of the archangels (in alphabetical order) and an overview of their purposes:

Ariel: *Heals and protects nature. At times placed as a fallen angel.*

Azrael: *Helps souls cross over. Angel of death in Islamic & Hebrew lore.*

Chamuel: *Angel of love. Lifts sorrow and improves relationships.*

Gabriel: *Messenger. Helps communication, leadership & intuition.*

Haniel: *Chief of angels, reveals healing secrets and keeps you centered.*

Jeremiel: *Reviews life after death. Aids psychic abilities and life changes.*

Jophiel: *Patron of artists, Illuminates creativity and aids in expression.*

Metatron: *Record keeper, supreme angel of death and guides children.*

Michael: *Provides safety, removes fear and helps fulfill life purpose.*

Raguel: *Resolves dispute, brings justice and oversees other archangels.*

Raphael: *Assists with healing, adapting a healthy lifestyle and travel.*

Raziel: *Knows the secrets of the Universe. Raises psychic understanding.*

Sandalphon: *Brother of Metatron. Brings prayers to God to be fulfilled.*

Uriel: *Guides ideas, inspiration and intelligence. Rebuilds after disasters.*

These archangels all understand, and work together to manifest the Order of the Universe in our daily lives. Sensing the presence of an angel doesn't require intuition. Often, it's simply recognizing the changes and support offered throughout our existence. The more you take time to recognize the presence of angels, the easier it will be for you to identify their individual energies. People often report feelings of tingling, vibration, warmth, safety and higher consciousness when in an angel's presence.

When calling on in angel, say its name three times in a row. While this step isn't completely necessary, the purpose is to help a higher being distinguish whether you are just thinking about them or if they are truly needed. Essentially, you make a point to speak to them directly.

If you are expecting to hear or feel an immediate response, do not be discouraged if it's takes longer than you had hoped. The more anxious you are, the more you have room for disconnect. The calmer are you are, the clearer your messages will be. It's easier for you to interpret messages when your mind is centered and focused.

Considering that most angels do not physically present themselves, it is important that you calm your mind so you can process the internal dialogue exchanged. Additionally, it is important to know that while all prayers are heard, not all prayers are answered. Often times, the things we want are not the things we need. Angels do know your intentions, so if you are simply asking to win the lottery, do not expect immediate results. If you want to ask for the tools to achieve success, however, this is entirely plausible.

The difference between humans and angels is that angels do not have the same free will that humans do. While we're fully capable of helping our neighbors (or even walking away from those in need), an angel's life is fully dedicated to service. With the ability to travel between worlds, they're able to heal, guide and protect from the other side. We all have angels and guardians that watch over us. If you ever need their help, all you have to do is ask.

Spirit Guides

As our life purpose on earth is to evolve spiritually, angels don't require incarnation in the physical world because they're already spiritually advanced. Guides on the other hand have lived human lives and are actually evolved human souls. While both angels and guides work to assist those in the physical world, the two are completely different species. Generally speaking, guides have lived many lives on earth whereas angels have not. While typically an angel is called upon, guides are with you on a day-to-day basis.

Before you incarnate on earth, you are matched with a spirit guide that's most capable of supporting you over the duration of your life contract. Working to help you manage obstacles and lessons, a guide constantly oversees you on your human journey.

Spirit guides constantly offer insight, many times in the form of your conscience. Have you ever had the feeling you shouldn't do something, then later looked back and wished you had listened to yourself? It's easy to dismiss that internal voice as imagination or call it a coincidence, but it's not.

Aside from acting as our conscience, spirit guides will also present themselves in the form of a "sign" which we often ask for. Many times, a guide will even intervene to keep you on your path. An example? You're running late to work and are speeding. Suddenly, you hit ever red light! While this can be a frustrating encounter, it might simply be your spirit guide protecting you from an accident you're not contracted to experience at the present time.

Remember, that though a spirit guide constantly works to enrich our life, we also have free will. It's when we don't listen to that internal voice that things have a tendency to go wrong; at which point our spirit guide's purpose is to simply get us through that rough patch. Keep in mind, some undesirable experiences are necessary for our souls to grow. It's times like these that our guides work from behind the scenes. Making sure we learn our lessons, a guide often uses difficult experiences to make major shifts that redirect us to where we need to be. The less we resist change and allow for these shifts, the faster our guides will get us back on track. Often, all this requires is a little trust and patience. The more open your mind is to the signs that are right in front of you, the faster you will benefit from the help they're readily available to provide.

NOTES

Chapter Two

Picturing animals or seeing them multiple times can mean more than you think.

ANIMAL SYMBOLOGY

Native American culture, dream analysis experts, and other ancient traditions, consider animal symbols a significant part of our day-to-day lives. Furthermore, a totem (spirit guide in the form of an animal) may present itself in both the dream state and while fully conscious. While animals are a regular occurrence, coming across one that is unusual, or seeing the same one several times may actually be a sign!

The following alphabetical guide includes a list of some common animals and the meanings of how they reflect your current situation. Keep in mind that interpretations may vary from one culture to another.

ANIMAL	MEANING
Aardvark	Be slow and cautious, but trust your instincts. Don't hide from your problems. You may also be avoiding social situations.
Alligator / Crocodile	It's a good time to set boundaries and be protective. Get in touch with yourself on a more primal level.
Ants	Begin looking at the bigger picture. Discipline, cooperation and patience are important at this time.
Badger	You may be dealing with someone who is nagging or interfering with your life. On the other hand, you may need to act more like a badger yourself; be persistent, stick to your gut no matter what and be more aggressive. It's a good time to be a leader and express your ideas and emotions.
Bat	Face your fears. Embrace rebirth! Stop playing it safe because you're not learning as much as you need to in order to grow.
Bear	Introspection, self-sufficiency and natural born leadership. Seeing a bear may also represent coming triumph.

Beaver	Take action. It might be a good time to put your dreams into motion or peruse home improvements. Don't neglect your teeth!
Bedbugs	Negative feelings or discomfort associated with sleeping arrangements (spouse, location, etc.) or bad sleeping patterns.
Bee	While bee's are self-sufficient, they also rely heavily on teamwork. Examine your productivity. It might be time to ask for help if you're feeling overwhelmed. Keep your eyes on the ~~honey~~ end prize.
Bird	Simple birds represent balance, peace, joy and freedom (or desire for those things).
Boa constrictor	You're in an overwhelming situation or relationship that's leaving you feeling powerless / constricted.
Buffalo	Remain grounded. Stay true to your character and be humble. Pray not only to ask for help, but to show gratitude as well.
Bugs / Flies	Small bugs represent irritation (generally in your daily life) while large bugs represent feeling vulnerable or fearful.
Bull	Narrow-mindedness and rapid decisions.
Butterfly	A reminder that who and where you are in life will transform with time. Look for joy and beauty in even the worst of situations.
Camel	Your body, mind and/or soul need to be replenished. Also, one of the only two symbols that represent total survival.
Cat	Desire or ability to be independent. Trust your own instincts rather than looking to those around you - but don't be antisocial.
Caterpillar	Have patience. Timing is everything.
Cattle	You're suffering from a lack of confidence or feel like you've lost your individuality – just like a herd of cattle.
Centaur	Struggle for balance internally. Duality in intellectual and physical behavior. Represents the animal nature in humans.

Chicken / Hen	If the chicken / hen is healthy, it represents fertility and balance. Don't be afraid to step outside of your comfort zone. If the chicken is ill or has its head cut off, it represents reluctance and a lack of courage.
Cockroach	Cockroaches are the second only symbol that represents complete survival. On the contrary, they can also represent major discomfort either mentally or physically.
Cow	Abundance and maternal instincts to earth.
Crab	Undergoing of a difficult experience and feelings of negativity from an external source. Feeling sensitive.
Crow	An omen of change. If you've been working towards something, it will soon be coming to fruition. Be mindful of your opinions and actions. You must be willing to walk your talk and speak the truth.
Deer	Be gentle with yourself and others. Do not push against the current. Be gentle and you will be nurtured in return.
Dinosaur	If you see a dinosaur, you are dealing with an overwhelming / highly demanding situation or old issues. If you are the dinosaur, it represents triumph over large struggles. Be careful not to be destructive.
Dog	Loyalty, love and protection. Evaluate the behaviors of the dog (or whose dog it is) to consider how it applies to your life.
Dolphin	Remember to listen more and talk less – not only to sounds, but to your body, the earth and others. Dolphins represent kindness, love, sensitivity and a connection with the universe.
Donkey	Don't misinterpret independence in others for being stubborn. Work hard and cooperate with others. Don't forget to set limits so that you don't exhaust yourself or others from working too hard.

Dove	Spiritual connections with creative or loving energy and the earth. The Dove is also a sign of peace, maternity and prophecy.
Dragon	Something difficult / untamed needs to be defeated. Realize your own potential so that you can transform and overcome obstacles.
Dragonfly	Inhabits two very different elements: air and water. Seeing a dragonfly encourages you to break bad habits and realize your potential. Water and air move; be willing to make change and be open to wisdom.
Duck / Goose	Represents taking comfort in your element and vulnerability. Learn to maneuver through challenges with grace and comfort.
Eagle / Falcon	Self-confidence and freedom (intellectually and physically). Eagles are a demanding symbol, but also bring great rewards. New beginnings, spiritual awakenings and opportunities are near! Falcons tell us to fully commit if we desire success. Take flight and soar with open-mindedness and grace.
Elephant	Either you are seeking wisdom or are surrounded by someone who has a lot of knowledge to offer you.
Firefly	A magical symbol of inspiration and hope. Also a symbol of spiritual awakening and reward. Have hope if things look dark.
Fish	Represents adaptation and an effort from the spiritual world to connect. Go with the flow and explore your creative side.
Fox	Someone in your company doesn't have your best interests at heart; they're cunning and cut-throat. This can also mean that as an individual you need to be more invisible and operate from behind our surroundings.
Frog / Toad	Don't allow yourself to be held down by life. Get in touch with your feelings and embrace transformation.

Animal	Meaning
Giraffe	Keep yourself grounded but don't get complacent - remain balanced. Be careful what you say to others as you can see a bigger picture from your point of view that they can't see on the ground.
Goat	Symbology behind the goat has long been debated. While many believe it's a symbol of lust and the devil, others see it as a sign of moving forward encouraging you to remain focused with a good work ethic.
Goldfish	You're in a restricting situation.
Gorilla	Remain grounded and ask yourself if you're being too materialistic. Your endeavors are solid, but examine your approach.
Grasshopper	Trust your instincts. If you take a leap of faith, you'll be rewarded with success. Also a sign of abundance / good luck to come.
Hippopotamus	A symbol of power, but the potential to lose control with it. Be careful to stay grounded. Represents healing and intuitive abilities.
Hornet	Represents a bad situation. Don't get stung!
Horse	You're at a crossroads in your journey. If you're feeling constricted, now is the time to travel in new directions. A symbol of courage, persistence and drive. Also a sign of sexual attraction and passion.
Hummingbird	Draw from natural resources for nutrition and medicine. A magical symbol to remind us of the powers within the earth. Try aroma therapy and detox your body of anger, anxiety and other negative energy. The hummingbird is also a symbol of love and your ability to freely spread joy.
Hyena	A cautionary message to choose your words and actions carefully – especially at work and within group settings.
Kangaroo	While kangaroos only move forward, this should be a reminder to do so as well. The catch? They're over-protective. Are you?

Kitten	Innocent intentions, but may also indicate feeling helpless if you're helping others in a difficult situation.
Koala	Consider incorporating eucalyptus into your routine. Also, be careful not to act out of emotional response (remain under control).
Ladybug	Someone is watching over you. Offering protection and good luck, a ladybug reminds us that annoyances will dissipate.
Leech	Be careful not to surround yourself with a freeloader. This person lacks self-respect and any sense of responsibility.
Leopard	Your body is purging attachments with trauma or demons from the past. This is also a sign of renewal, communication and raising of your awareness / unconscious.
Lice	You need to cleanse yourself of emotional, physical or spiritual negativity. If you're feeling easily irritable, this is why.
Lion / Tiger	Strength of character, loyalty and leadership. If you're waiting for resolution, you will see victory. Be fearless and relax.
Lizard	Symbolizes death followed by resurrection. This is not always "physical death" - When a lizard loses its tail it regenerates; you too can shed and rebuild to achieve your goals. Also, analyze your dream meanings more.
Locus	Something meant to help you achieve your destiny has been disturbed. Vengeance may be coming into your life.
Maggot	You may be acting selfishly or to gain from other people's efforts. Begin considering how you can serve others more often.
Mockingbird	You may be lacking individual expression or dealing with an adulterous partner. Look inside yourself instead of looking outward.
Monkey	A symbol of duality in human nature. See both sides of light and dark in everything so that your perspective remains true.

Mouse	If you're feeling disorganized or scrutinized, you may be paying too much attention to details. Stop over-analyzing.
Octopus	Though a sign of the underworld, it primarily reflects memories, creation and power. A reminder that you can accomplish more than the average person in an efficient way if you use your intelligence.
Ostrich	Simplify your life and be more practical.
Owl	Great wisdom and knowledge. Tap into your observational skills and you will heighten you intuition and clairvoyant gifts.
Parrot	Know when to speak and when to remain silent. You may not be thinking for yourself as much as you think you are.
Peacock	You're dealing with karmic debt and the situations in your life reflect that. Be careful not to be arrogant or too self-loving. If you recognize the changes that need to be made, you will have a beautiful rebirth.
Pegasus	Vitality. You have the strength of a horse and the freedom or weightlessness of a bird. You have the capacity to overcome much in the physical world and inspire. Your gift is transforming evil into good.
Penguin	Seeing penguins is a sign that you're actually spending time in the astral plane (generally while asleep). You have the unique ability to travel between dimensions both when you're awake and asleep.
Phoenix	You're capable of bouncing back from anything! A huge sign of rebirth. You're closer to achieving complete spiritual awareness than ever before.
Pig	You may be taking more than you need. This is also a good time to cleanse yourself with sage and take a long bath.
Porcupine	You or someone else is acting defensively. Also a sign of over sensitivity.

Praying Mantis	Hypocrisy could be prevented if patient.
Rabbit	Take more time to plan and approach things more methodically. You may be too physically or sexually obsessive, frustrated or preoccupied. Shift your focus from flaws and satisfaction to responsibility.
Raccoon	Now is a good time to disguise and transform yourself so that you can accomplish what you need to.
Racehorse	Representative of your underlying competitive nature and want to excel in your desires or to get ahead.
Rats	Ask yourself if you're pushing too hard or not hard enough to get what you want. Adapt to your surroundings to avoid confrontation and don't let yourself get too aggressive or manipulative.
Scorpion	Triumph over death or hardship. In times of transformation however, whether the change is calm or chaotic is entirely up to you. Scorpions also represent death of ideas, relationships and habits.
Seahorse	You may be living in a fairytale land and need to ground yourself. Also a sign of sacrifice and concern for others.
Shark	Pay careful attention to your senses. Meditation is essential at this time. Trust your instincts about people and work.
Skunk	Give respect to get respect. Recognize your own qualities in order to learn and grow. You have the ability to sexually attract people or tendency to completely push them away. Find balance.
Snake	If dealing with people, be careful of cleverness. If in hardship, you will soon shed your skin and enter a new chapter. You're capable of experiencing things without resistance, but you must gauge the situation to see if you're in danger.

Spider	A warning against temptation but also a sign to peruse artistic endeavors.
Squirrel	Conserve your energy and evaluate what you've gathered that's cluttering your life versus what's essential. You're likely taking on too much at a time, so be sure to make time to socialize and relax.
Stork	Birth; either of a child, new idea, job or emotion. This is a sign of fertility and creation. It's time to reconnect with family.
Swan	Realize your inner and outer beauty. Pay attention to your hunches. Make sure that your relationships are mutual. Allow yourself not only to give, but to receive gifts and healing willingly.
Turkey	Prepare to receive spiritual, monetary or intellectual gifts. You will soon feel a sense of abundance.
Turtle	The oldest symbol of the earth. Total energy and connection with the universe. Honor and ground yourself to the planet. Be mindful of your creativity and the limitless possibilities.
Unicorn	Your spirit is in the process of healing and restoring so that your dreams can come true. Explore your spiritual potential.
Wolf	An indication of your spirit guides presence. One of the biggest symbols that your intuition is strengthening. Explore your inner power. Let go of physical attachments in exchange for emotional and spiritual growth. Harmony comes with discipline.
Zebra	A representation of the duality you poses. You may also be fighting to maintain your individuality or feel like you stand out too much from the crowd. This is a symbol of polarity and need for balance. Remember that things are rarely black and white.

Applying Animal Symbology

In my experience, animal symbology is most helpful when you're already looking for something specific. The best way I can describe this is like buying a new car. I frequently see people notice cars "just like theirs" or "just like the one they wanted" once they get a new vehicle. If you just purchased a red SUV for example, noticing more red SUVs does not imply that there's actually more of them on the road – it's a reflection that you're seeing more of what is now a part of your life (you now have a reason to look for them). The same can be said for buying a car and seeing more of the one you wanted to purchase (but didn't) or looking to buy a car and seeing the ones you're considering buying. With animal symbology, it's a lot like buying a car. The animal kingdom doesn't radically change overnight – but when your life changes, you're more prone to see certain animals which often reflect the situations and emotions you're experiencing. Furthermore, as you continue to invest energy in building your spiritual self, certain animals will present themselves because you can now benefit from their meanings as you're more receptive to their messages.

The most beneficial times to look up an animal's significance is when you see one that is out of the ordinary, or if you see the same kind of animal several times. If you ever have that random moment where a "shark" crosses your mind, that might also be a good opportunity to see what it means! Taking into consideration the connotations we've adapted with certain animals, it's easy to understand why you might see more snake jewelry or tattoos in a week when you're experiencing a situation with someone who's "acting like a snake".

However you decide to apply Animal Symbolgy to your life, make an effort to set aside your reservations and honestly acknowledge the times it feels important to look up an animal's meaning. Even the times you don't connect with a description, ask yourself if it could be attached to a repressed emotion or perhaps a message from your guides about a situation. Utilize the following few pages to reflect on your animal encounters. This can be helpful when you see something that doesn't seem significant at the time. While you're facing things head on it can be difficult to see the bigger picture. Reflecting after a situation has passed, you might be able to see what it was you initially missed. With future situations this will help you learn what to look for.

ANIMAL JOURNAL

STEVEN BINKO

ANIMAL JOURNAL

ANIMAL JOURNAL

Chapter Three

Achieving a higher frequency and collective consciousness. The birth of our new reality.

ASCENSION

As a race, humans are constantly evolving. Our bodies are physically capable of adapting immunities to medicine and our chemistry changes as the atmosphere and earth change. Mentally, our perception is mutable and constantly develops with each life experience. Spiritually however, we're in an age which every aspect of our being is undergoing a transformative process. The blueprint for the human race is rapidly evolving to a higher frequency and consciousness. This evolution to a higher state of being is called ascension; our rebirth into a new reality.

The ascension process raises our energy and enhances our spiritual awareness. While we each transform at a different rate, those who are more open-minded will adapt faster and may bypass certain emotional, physical and spiritual symptoms. Imagine your body as if it were a car. If you're the kind of person who performs routine maintenance, getting an oil change is nothing out of the ordinary. If you're the kind of person who waits until your dashboard fills up with warning lights, your car is more prone to stalling on the road - accompanied by emotional frustration. In this scenario, your body is a vehicle for your spiritual journey; those who actively seek to improve their life and who are open-minded will have a smoother ride.

Though interpretations of the ascension process vary, many world traditions and religions recognize the shift. In Buddhism, the profound revelation of life's meaning is called Enlightenment. In Christianity, the word Ascension is actually a biblical term that describes when Christ's body resurrected and went from earth into the heavens.

In watching the news, you will find a clear contrast between those who are awakening and those who are still spiritually dormant. The people who are not spiritually evolving are the same beings that contribute to the turmoil within the world; they do not recognize the value of human life and a higher purpose. Many times, the clearest indicators that a person is "dormant" are ego, judgment and pride – all of which are contributing factors in global corruption.

When researching the ascension process, it's easy to feel overwhelmed. As people around the world begin to make this transition, the ideas and understanding surrounding the ascension process are constantly evolving (potentially leaving you with conflicting information). The important thing to remember is that each person is undergoing their own enlightenment process; some will transition faster and perceptions will vary, dependent upon how spiritually developed an individual already is. Like a red painting, two people may look at the same artwork and interpret two completely different emotions; one may see love, the other could see hate. The same should be applied to this evolution. As we're each on a different spiritual path, the ways in which we achieve our awakening will also differ.

Though the concept of balance remains consistent in many spiritual teachings, it's important to note this is not the case with the final destination in ascension. Negativity will no longer serve a purpose to those who have already learned from and released it. The result of this evolution is a more compassionate and creative society working together as a collective consciousness through divine wisdom. Ascension is about transforming negative into positive, fear into courage, selfishness into selflessness, prejudice into acceptance and cruelty into compassion - all means by which corruption can thrive will be removed.

Considering the ascension process has already started, you may find yourself asking what will happen to those who haven't begun spiritually awakening or ascending yet. First, those who do not ascend are not being punished. Spiritually, we all have different contracts. Many young souls (people will few life incarnations – not physical age) are simply inexperienced in raising their vibration. Additionally, young souls often live in a fear based mentality which will ultimately prevent them from embracing the change. While the people who don't ascend will likely experience major shifts and disasters on earth, this is simply for their growth and essential to shift mass numbers of people at the same time.

For those who do not immediately ascend, the global tragedies they will experience allow them to quickly move from the physical realm (where they can no longer profit from a 3D experience) to the fourth dimension where they will be guided in achieving spiritual transformation and complete ascension. It removes the need for further incarnations to evolve. While this chapter won't specifically detail the experience, understand that the transition described shouldn't be feared. Just as some religions believe in "Purgatory", it's not something to be feared; rather a state of being which allows for purification and growth in "holiness" to then ascend to "heaven".

Like a computer downloading an update, your ascension progress takes time and may require several stages. Depending on the person, you may experience a variety of symptoms for days or weeks at a time. Your mind, body and soul are all making major changes, so it's natural to notice side-effects as you adjust and settle in to your new state of being. Remember that this process is different for everyone so the degree of side-effects and number of "upgrades" will vary drastically between individuals. In the table below, check off any symptoms you've been experiencing to help you determine if you might be spiritually awakening or beginning the ascension process already.

	Random moments of crying or laughter for no apparent reason
	Increased connection with nature or sensitivity towards animals
	Feeling "out of place" or like you're living in an alternate reality
	Extreme sensitivity to sound where small noises feel amplified
	Hearing ringing or muffled pulsating sounds more than usual
	Decreased perception of time or feeling like "time is running out"
	The sudden desire to simplify your house, wardrobe, clutter, etc.
	Spouts of confusion, disorientation or feeling spaced out
	Unusual headaches/sensations that don't respond to medicine
	Tingling in your fingertips, crown of your head or behind the ears
	Increased moments of Déjà vu
	Unexplained nervousness & anxiety / unusual internal vibrations
	Heightened intuition, prophetic dreams, enhanced psychic ability
	Periods of extreme fatigue despite full night of sleep
	Random spouts of energy despite lack of sleep
	Waking up at weird hours for no apparent reason (ie. 2am - 4am)
	Electronics malfunction or act strange by touch / with mood shifts
	Having complex thoughts that you understand but can't verbalize
	New emotional resistance towards certain foods / eating habits
	Having a gut feeling like "something big is going to happen"
	Unusual change in bowl movements and digestion
	More vivid dreaming or complete dream amnesia after waking

	Flu like symptoms that appear and disappear without getting sick
	Noticing a haze, light or auras around people, plants or animals
	Sudden desire for alone time (even though not depressed)
	Frequent coincidences or re-occurring numbers
	You can't explain it, but you feel weird - like you're "not yourself"
	Feel like you can't breathe deep enough because of chest tension
	Seeing random flashes of light / shadows in peripheral vision
	Feel like your body is expanding – pressure or coordination is off
	Moments of profound (unexplained) connection with new people
	Strong (random) desire to move or change jobs without thought
	Difficulty deciphering real from imagined events & conversations
	Wondering how you got somewhere / what you were looking for
	Random changes in heart rate or unusual heart palpitations
	Feel you're floating from your body while attempting to fall asleep
	Change in perspective you can't explain – deep sense of knowing
	Feel resistance to watching the news, movies or negative music
	Unusual spontaneity with things you normally wouldn't consider
	Shift of mentality - complex things suddenly feel very simple
	Moments of telepathy with other people (thoughts or feelings)
	Loss of depth perception or things appearing closer than they are
TOTAL	/ 42

Disclaimer: While experiencing a majority of the side-effects listed above is a good indication that you're experiencing awakening or ascension, they may also be the result of a medical condition. Please consult a health care professional as needed.

What to expect after ascending

Even though each person's experience may vary, the foundation of this new life remains consistent. Like driving through a thick fog, the veil between dimensions will slowly be lifted the closer you get.

Upon ascending, the first thing many people will notice is a change in their appearance. You will project yourself in the physical form of your most confident self-image - any age, sex, ethnicity, build, etc. This is not to say you're a completely different person - you still retain your memories (free of negative emotions) and personality. Physically aging becomes optional as time no longer exists. Put simply, you're no longer a soul trapped in a human body; you are your soul projecting itself in the most comfortable human-like form. It's the religious equivalent of taking on an "angel" form. High dimensions can't support physicality.

As you begin your experience in higher dimensions, many of the material attachments and earthly distractions you encountered will dissipate. "Work" in the new realm will be on a volunteer basis (acts of servitude and selflessness) and "jobs" will no longer have the same significance they did on earth. You may even work as a spirit guide.

The most significant change is the adaptation of a group consciousness. Thoughts, feelings and emotions will be shared and understood with ease. There is no judgment or need to explain yourself as everyone collectively understands each other. While it might seem weird that someone else could "tap into your thoughts", remember that your views in these higher dimensions are no longer pre-occupied with the same concerns you had on earth. Instead, the divine knowledge you're "downloaded" with directs your thoughts, intentions and behaviors.

Before ascending, you may have struggled to accomplish ideas or goals you set for yourself – this will no longer be the case. Humans were not designed to live lives of suffering. Suffering is something mankind has done to itself. In the third dimension (earth), we were fortunate enough to have a time delay between our thoughts and manifestation (the law of attraction.) Once you have ascended, anything you think will immediately manifest itself. This is one of the many reasons some people don't immediately ascend. Imagine what it would be like for someone who is angry, resentful or fear based to immediately manifest their thoughts and emotions into physical form. These people still have soul-growth to accomplish on lower dimensions before joining you in a higher dimension. Even though you could manifest your dream house or car, your attachment to these material things will be long gone as you embrace your new way of living. Most of what you desire to manifest will be for a higher good. If you're concerned about ascending, begin transforming your thoughts and practice manifesting things on the third dimension. Stop thinking what it would be like to "someday have the things you desire" as the universe will continue to return it that way - something that will always be in the future. Begin outputting your energy as if you already have what you desire so it will return that way.

On the third dimension, we've learned to label things as right or wrong. As you strive for spiritual growth and awakening, release this way of thinking and discharge the desire to "fix" things - accept they just ARE. Humans have created the illusion of light and dark, when in reality, everything is light. The appearance of "dark" is simply to provide us a contrast so that we can more easily identify what we truly need, as well as appreciate what we already have. When we hold onto the "contrast", we're not capable of receiving that which is truly for our higher good. It's when we release that which we hold onto that we can truly embrace our full potential and receive that which is good.

Reading about those who do not immediately ascend, you might feel worried you'll be left out of this new utopian world. Try to stop that thought process and immediately shift your consciousness to improving your current way of living. The more you commit yourself, the faster you accelerate your individual ascension process. Our behavioral patterns are directly parallel with our progress in ascending.

Despite potential for incredible experiences that the earth possesses, it's important not to get too attached to the physical world. When you find yourself too consumed by what's happening in your life, take a moment to meditate and release yourself. Life on earth is a blink in time compared to what's ahead. As long as you live your life to its fullest potential you have nothing to worry about. While in physical form, do the "maintenance" and continually look for ways to improve your mental, physical and spiritual health.

Ascended Masters

Historically, it is recorded that the Ascended Masters have worked with humankind for centuries. An Ascended Master is a being who raised their vibration, achieved enlightenment and serves humanity. Though they were "ordinary" humans in past incarnations, an Ascended Master has a complete understanding of our universal connection and purpose beyond their own existence; they did not live in the ego-based mentality that most of mankind operates from. In Christianity, Jesus Christ is a great example of an Ascended Master. Jesus aside, there are many masters who are not religious figures.

Ascended Masters serve as teachers to mankind in a variety of ways from the spirit realm. In your journey towards ascension, these beings aid in your spiritual growth and journey towards enlightenment. Though they no longer walk this dimension in 3D form, the Ascended Masters are constantly working to inspire, motivate and aid us in recognizing our spiritual selves. On your journey towards Ascension, you may call on the Ascended Masters at any given time. For those who do not ascend, the Ascended Masters will serve as teachers in the 4th dimension afterlife to aid in the eventual ascension to the 5th dimension and higher. In the most simple of terms, Ascended Masters have already undergone and completed the spiritual journey we are currently undergoing. It is their goal and purpose to help us achieve the same awakening and ascension towards a universal consciousness.

It is a sad truth, but humanity has been programed to resist many of the ideas and resources that ultimately serve in helping it to ascend. The Ascended Masters have unbelievable amounts of compassion, love and wisdom to serve humanity. As a species, it is essential that we open our mind and call on their help to access the unlimited and unconditional resources available. The ascension process has already begun!

NOTES

NOTES

Chapter Four

Travel anywhere in the universe
without leaving the house.

ASTRAL PROJECTION

At one point or another, it's likely you've heard stories about someone who had a "near death experience" (NDE) or "out of body experience" (OBE). Reports of these incidents date back thousands of years and range from seeing the "tunnel of white light" to witnessing one's own surgery from outside the physical body. Though both OBE's and NDE's often happen as a result of a traumatic experience or in the dream state, there's actually a way to voluntarily travel in the same dimension at your own discretion – Astral Projection.

Beyond your 3D reality, there's an unlimited number of experiences and dimensions available for you to explore! By consciously releasing the soul (Astral Body) from the physical body, you can travel to anywhere in the universe. Like a rental car, your body is simply a temporary house for your soul energy. The physical body was provided to you as a catalyst for your soul to encounter the experiences necessary to grow.

Connected to the physical body by an energetic cord, astral traveling allows the astral body to project itself / function independently while retaining memory of the experience. When astral projecting, the 4th dimension is encountered. Here, qualities of the 3rd dimension remain consistent, though the senses are greatly amplified and many of the earthly laws (like gravity) no longer apply.

The astral dimension operates at a much higher frequency than the physical realm and can be broken down into three levels – low, middle and high astral planes. The lower astral plane operates at a slightly higher frequency than the vibration experienced in 3D (life on earth). Comparatively, this level is very similar to what you might encounter in the dream state and is also the most common place for astral travel. It is the easiest to accomplish and the one this chapter will outline techniques for accessing. The middle and high dimensions of the astral plane can closely be compared to the religious interpretation of "heaven". Finding documentation to describe the detail of these planes remains limited as people often struggle to find the vocabulary to describe the experience. On a human level, we don't have the capacity to understand or explain what is encountered. Getting to a higher plane through basic techniques is possible but requires knowledge of raising your own frequency. It's important to note that traveling on the higher astral planes is not like taking an elevator; there is no clear distinction between "floors". Often, travelers unknowingly float between levels and are able to encounter characteristics experienced in the higher dimensions such as time distortion and angels.

The advantage of astral travel is the ability to experience life beyond your physical senses or limitations. Imagine traveling to any country or planet. Through greater experiences, we are more emotionally capable of understanding our purpose as our perception of reality enriches. We can then see the bigger picture. The restraints of 3D life (example: money) do not apply on the astral plane either; there's no cost to travel. You can fly anywhere you want with your astral body. On the 4th dimension, you're also able to speak directly with your guides. Many people even astral travel to meet deceased loved ones or enhance their psychic abilities.

Throughout your time in the astral plane, you will notice a cord that connects you to your physical body. Often a blue, silver or white pulsating cord, this connection cannot be broken. No matter how far you go, you are always capable of returning to your physical body. This is also the way that both the astral and physical bodies can communicate in the event they need to rejoin. As an example, if your physical body were in danger due to a house fire, your astral body would immediately receive that information through this cord (most likely by utilizing your senses or by immediately pulling you back to your body). Each person has this cord that connects the body to its soul – the only variations are cord colors and where the cord connects. The most common places people see their cord connection are their belly button area, the center of their forehead and from the heart. The only time this connection can be broken is when you die. For that, no one can "enter your body" while you are astral traveling.

While on the astral plane, it's likely you will see other people and souls. Some people enjoy astral traveling alone, while others prefer to share a group experience with friends, family or a romantic partner. Talk about a cheap honeymoon! Aside from those who are also astral traveling, you're now in a dimension where you can see souls that have "crossed over" as well as those who are lucid dreaming. Lucid dreaming is very similar to astral projection, and in many senses it's the same thing. When someone becomes aware that they're dreaming, they're able to take control of the environment and manifest what they see and where they go. The only significant difference between astral projection and lucid dreaming is that a person who is lucid dreaming becomes conscious while already out of the body, whereas astral projection allows you to consciously go from a waking-state to out-of-body state. Additionally, those lucid dreaming may visualize imaginary variables as they transition from the dream state into the astral plane. Both require immense relaxation, which is why those who are dreaming can so easily "waken" their astral bodies and begin astral traveling. Whichever method is used to accomplish this voluntary out of body experience, many people find they are more "awake" when they're "asleep" as they are finally able to see life beyond their own physical existence.

Astral Projection Methods

There are literally hundreds of ways to achieve astral projection. In this chapter, you will find some of the more basic methods. Remember that even the "easy" ways take practice, so do not be discouraged if it takes you a while to achieve your first successful projection. Additionally, you may want to start with a small goal (example: go from your bedroom to your bathroom) and slowly work towards further destinations.

Lucid Breakthrough

Many dreams stem from thoughts initiated earlier in the day or from the last thing thought about while attempting to fall asleep. Throughout the day, make a point to tell yourself that you're going to have a lucid dream (becoming aware you are dreaming and taking control of your dream). Do this all day and as you try to fall asleep. You are essentially programming your subconscious to induce a lucid dream. Once you are in a lucid dream (know that you are dreaming), you will either know that you're no longer in your body or be able to leave your physical body. Your dream-land will likely disappear and you will see yourself above your physical body.

Anchoring

While lying down, become aware of your entire body by tightening and then relaxing each muscle. Starting with your toes and work upwards towards the crown of your head. As you release your muscle in each part of your body, feel the area get heavier and heavier. The goal in mind is to visualize yourself sinking out of your physical body. While this is one of the more commonly used methods, some people "snap" back into their body as soon as they feel the sinking sensation. It can be compared to feeling like you're going to fall off your bed when you're about to fall asleep. With practice however, you will teach yourself to trust the feeling.

The Helium Effect

Visualize the white body of light that resides within you. Now, imagine slowly attaching hundreds of balloons to various parts of your astral body. Be aware of how dense your physical body feels in contrast to the lightness and lifting of your astral body. Eventually, you will lift up and out!

Sit-Up

Try to visualize your astral body sitting up while your physical body remains laid down. At first, you may become frustrated with the resistance to elevate your back. If this happens, it's recommended you try another method, as the frustration will likely make you focus too heavily as opposed to relaxing.

Pull-Up Rope

Become totally aware of your hands and arms. Do not see your limbs as separate entities. Instead, recognize how they are connected to your body. Now, visualize an imaginary rope hanging from the celling and imagine your astral hands pulling your astral body up on the rope. Continue to do this until you are fully out of your physical body.

Tips

Whichever method you use, there are some general guidelines that can be followed to help you achieve astral projection faster. The most important thing is to make sure that you are fully relaxed. To do this, some people prefer to attempt projection in the nude so they don't feel restricted (or bound) to their bodies by the clothing material. Also, if you're exhausted, it's very easy to end up falling asleep. For this, some people prefer to attempt astral projection upon waking up while they're still groggy/relaxed, but rested enough they won't fall back asleep. If you've just eaten a huge meal or if you're feeling hungry, you will also be more focused on your stomach and body which prevents your mind from relaxing. Lastly, the most important thing is to release fears and doubts. The moment you begin to fear anything, your astral body will attempt to protect itself by attaching to your physical body as a defense mechanism. Do not doubt yourself or put too much pressure on achieving this the first try. Sit back, relax and have fun!

Additional Exercises

1. Have someone write a number on a piece of paper in another room without you seeing what they wrote. Astral travel to where they've placed the paper and write the number down when you return to your physical body. Compare the numbers to verify if you were dreaming or actually astral traveling.

2. Travel with a partner and compare experiences. See how similar or different your experiences were.

3. Journey to a friend's house before meeting with them later in the day. Make a note of what they're wearing so you can verify it when you see them later.

4. Astral Travel to a restaurant or location you've wanted to visit but haven't seen yet. Try to remember as many details about the place as possible. When you return to your physical body, write the details down and then visit the location to validate.

PROGRESS LOG

PROGRESS LOG

Chapter Five

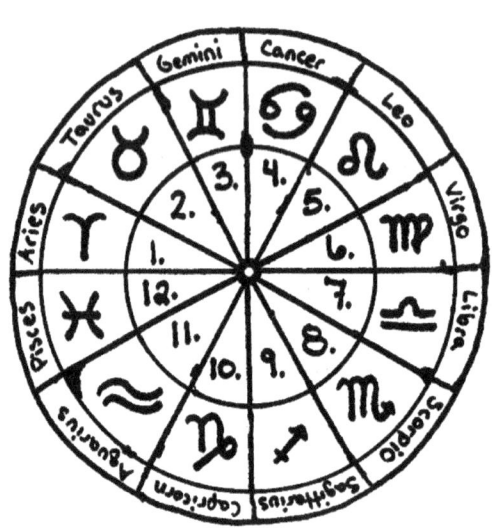

1 Mar 21 - Apr 19	**2** Apr 20 - May 20	**3** May 21 - Jun 21
4 Jun 22 - Jul 22	**5** Jul 23 - Aug 22	**6** Aug 23 - Sep 22
7 Sep 23 - Oct 22	**8** Oct 23 - Nov 21	**9** Nov 22 - Dec 21
10 Dec 22 - Jan 19	**11** Jan 20 - Feb 18	**12** Feb 19 - Mar 20

What do the stars and planets say about you?
Learn how the cosmos affect your life!

ASTROLOGY

Astrology is one of the oldest forms of divination. By studying the planets and stars you can see how their movement and patterns affect your day to day life. This chapter reviews some of the basics.

In earlier years, some researchers believed that astrology lacked scientific evidence. Most recently however, studies have shown that the position of the moon and other planets has a dramatic effect on the earth, our thoughts and human behavior. The side of the earth, which faces the moon for example, is most prone to experiencing high tide. Bodies of water are easily affected by the gravitational pull. That taken into account, consider that your body is made up mostly by water. The moons position and gravitational pull can therefore affect you.

By examining the time and location of your birth, you can better understand your personality traits and behaviors. Even though your qualities aren't determined solely by your astrological chart, it can help you gain insight into your strengths, weaknesses and compatibility with others at home, work or in romantic relationships.

Zodiac Signs

About 2,500 years ago, the Babylonians developed a chart that divides the position of the stars. Corresponding with certain constellations, these 12 parts were named the signs of the zodiac. The illustration on the left can help you determine which sign you are. The twelve signs are: Aries *(The Ram)*, Taurus *(The Bull)*, Gemini *(The Twins)*, Cancer *(The Crab)*, Leo *(The Lion)*, Virgo *(The Maiden)*, Libra *(The Scales)*, Scorpio *(The Scorpion)*, Sagittarius *(The Archer)*, Capricorn *(The Goat)*, Aquarius *(The Water-bearer)* and Pisces *(The Fish)*.

While Zodiac signs vary in some countries, the 12 signs included in this book are the most widely accepted. In Chinese culture for example, the signs aren't divided by month or derived from constellations. The year in which you were born would decide which of their signs you are.

Ruling Planets

According to Western Astrology, each zodiac sign's characteristics are influenced from one planet (called a ruling planet). The following chart will show you each sign and the planet it is ruled by:

SIGN	RULING PLANET
Aries	Mars
Taurus	Venus
Gemini	Mercury
Cancer	Moon
Leo	Sun
Virgo	Mercury
Libra	Venus
Scorpio	Pluto (co-ruled by Mars)
Sagittarius	Jupiter
Capricorn	Saturn
Aquarius	Uranus (co-ruled by Saturn)
Pisces	Neptune (co-ruled by Jupiter)

It is the energies of the planets and their positions that influence many of the qualities appointed to a particular sign. As you begin to recognize a planets influence, it will help you understand how to utilize its energy! Here are some of the qualities associated with the ruling planets:

PLANET	INFLUENCE / QUALITIES
Jupiter	Luck, inspiration and greater fortune
Mars	Sexuality, motivation and ambition
Mercury	Communication, intellect, awareness and reasoning
Moon	Emotions, relationships and habits
Neptune	Illusion, dreams, spirituality, art and addiction
Pluto	Power, transformation/rebirth, destruction and crime
Saturn	Karma, discipline and responsibility
Sun	Giver of life, personality, ego and creativity
Uranus	Rebellion, individuality and originality
Venus	Pleasure, relationships, friendships and money

Elements & Mutability

The four elements (air, earth, fire and water) all apply to the basic nature and temperamental characteristics of the Zodiac signs in Astrology. Each elements has very distinct characteristics.

Elements

Fire: *Very energetic, passionate and fearless*
Earth: *Down to earth and practical in thinking*
Air: *Considerate, aware of others and intellectual*
Water: *Sensitive emotionally, intuitively and romantically*

Qualities

Cardinal: *Independent, proactive and impatient*
Fixed: *Determined, dependable and un-changing/consistent*
Mutable: *Adaptable/flexible, Spontaneous and Impulsive*

If you were born on the cusp of a different sign, it's very possible that you will possess qualities of the sign close to yours. The following chart shows each sign, their element and their mutability:

SIGN	ELEMENT	QUALITY
Aries	Fire	Cardinal
Taurus	Earth	Fixed
Gemini	Air	Mutable
Cancer	Water	Cardinal
Leo	Fire	Fixed
Virgo	Earth	Mutable
Libra	Air	Cardinal
Scorpio	Water	Fixed
Sagittarius	Fire	Mutable
Capricorn	Earth	Cardinal
Aquarius	Air	Fixed
Pisces	Water	Mutable

Aries
March 21 – April 19

Typically, the Aries assumes leadership roles and initiates progress when something needs to be accomplished. Though they're quick to get things going, Aries downfall is they may have a hard time completing tasks they've started. Socially, they're very good at getting people to take part in their causes; they're charming and good at motivating others. Like their symbol (the Ram), Aries is strong in character which can be misinterpreted by more sensitive or non-confrontational zodiac signs. Bold in nature, it may seem at times they're stubborn or unwilling to see another's viewpoint, but it is also this quality that helps them stand their ground when it comes to matters of character. The Aries will take any problem head on and is very courageous. It is this competitive nature that fuels their leadership tendencies. Be careful however not to challenge an Aries authority; they'll stand behind their opinion even if they're wrong simply for the sake of having the last word. Even though the Aries works hard, they are fearless along the way and always make time for play.

Taurus
April 20 – May 20

The Taurus loves comfort in every sense of the word. From material belongings and success to the security of a relationship, the Taurus works hard to maintain the small luxuries in life. Despite how much they value their relationships, Taurus are a fixed sign and are extremely stubborn. A Taurus is persistent in finding efficient ways to accomplish what they set their mind to. Working hard for what they have, the Taurus strives to attain stability in the areas of their life. While this practicality can be useful at times, the Taurus can also fail to take on new ideas (or take on too many ideas) as they constantly assess risk. While very sentimental, loyal and sensual with a significant other, they can be easily frustrated if the same is not reciprocated. The Taurus is strong-willed and enjoys challenging themselves to do better and accomplish more. Be patient with this sign. Even though they may come off "obsessive" or "bull headed", their intentions are in the right place and they'll be by your side to the end.

Gemini
May 21 – June 21

A very sociable (and flirtatious) sign, the Gemini is quick to share what's on their mind. Constantly searching for meaning in their thoughts and experiences, the Gemini gets much of its fulfillment from intellectual growth. As a result of their thoughtful nature, the Gemini can assess social settings and bring life to the party. When it comes to balance, a Gemini is great at seeing both sides of the story which is also their downfall. Being that they can see both potential outcomes, the Gemini cans struggle to be decisive. Ultimately, many of a Gemini's decisions will be made based on trying to go with the flow. Along the way, their moods have potential to shift as fast as their environment does – for better or for worse. With their mind in so many places, a Gemini can be scatterbrained, but don't misinterpret that as them not caring or having ulterior motives. While a Gemini rarely assumes leadership positions, they're a valuable team member in offering a rounded perspective on almost any issue and communicate/debate effectively. Gemini also have a natural talent for being a great companion.

Cancer
June 22 – July 22

Maternal and domestic, the Cancer is known for taking comfort in home and family affairs. Maintaining both tradition and harmony is important to a Cancer. Though they can get emotional easily and have a hard time hiding their feelings, don't take Cancer's sensitivity for granted or they'll withdrawal quickly. Like their symbol (the crab), once they retreat into their shell, it can be very frustrating trying to get them to come back out. Eventually, they'll return to normal on their own accord. Known for their sensitivity, it's hard to reject a Cancer from what they want – but if you do, they're not above using emotional manipulation to get what they desired in the first place; they'll turn on the tears at the flip of a switch. Being as sensitive and sentimental as they are, these qualities are the foundation of life for a Cancer and the reason protecting friends or family is a high priority. Pay attention to what a Cancer gives emotionally, because they're more selfless than you'll ever know. Cancer aren't driven by belongings; all they desire is harmony at home.

About Leo
July 23 – August 22

Creative, extroverted and ambitious, Leo's quickly assume positions of showmanship. Leo are a common sign for those in the entertainment industry; they rarely shy away from attention for what they do best. The symbol for Leo is the Lion. Strong and determined, they're big on assuming positions of power or leadership and work hard to finish what they start. On the flip side, this strong and persistent persona can also feel domineering. A Leo is strong in their opinions and set in their ways which can be annoying, but great if you're looking for someone to back you up. The self-confidence and fearlessness makes for a great friend or teammate, but avoid having a Leo as your enemy! Leo's love to have a good time and excel when their abilities are challenged. As a romantic partner, the Leo is devoted and often sexually creative. Depending on who they're matched with, the passion can be extraordinary or too much to handle. Maybe it's their creative nature and ambition? Either way, a Leo commonly integrates fun with their drive to succeed.

Virgo
August 23 – September 22

Born to serve others, Virgo's pay close attention to detail and find their joy in doing so. Practical in their thinking, a Virgo takes great pride in getting things done right the first time. Though they're good at being grounded, the Virgo can be analytical or skeptical to a fault. If you want to get their attention or open their mind, use their thirst for knowledge to your advantage. Even when they don't agree with your perspective, they desire to understand your thoughts and feelings. As a worrywart, the Virgo is good at avoiding undesirable situations, though it is this same quality that can stifle their potential for new experiences. Socially and romantically, if you can get a Virgo to open up about their feelings, they will become devoted to the relationship. Be careful though; it's that vulnerability that can make them feel jealous as well. All in all, the Virgo often lead lives of servitude and excel when they're in a position to pay attention to detail. Despite the sometimes "restrictive" way of thinking, see the Virgo's intentions and be patient. They can provide great contrast to over-the-top ideas and are genuinely sincere.

Libra
September 23 – October 22

Team players in every sense of the word, Libras thrive on having various types of relationships. While some would call Libra "people pleasers", Libra just want things to be fair and balanced – hence their symbol, the scales. In attempt to do what's best for everyone, the Libra are famous for avoiding conflict at all costs. Additionally, it is this desire to satisfy everyone that makes Libra look indecisive at times, but they're really just highly compassionate. Being that they're generally sociable and cultured, Libra are great with coordinating social gatherings. It's quite important that the Libra stay active and have social opportunities to motivate them or they can become lazy. Libra are generally thoughtful and prefer to be surrounded by people who are knowledgeable. Even though they're sociable, Libra have a tendency to lack energy at work if they're missing the social factor. It is their social openness and quest for fairness that makes them a good romantic partner or co-worker. Open to compromise and unlikely to be manipulative, you pretty much get what you see when it comes to Libra.

Scorpio
October 23 – November 21

When it comes to the Scorpio, these people are on a mission! Whether they're looking to get to the bottom of things or are simply feeling curious, Scorpio are always searching for something. Using their keen sense of intuition, Scorpio often have faith in their decisions and prefer to take control of their own destiny. Being fearless, independent and determined to succeed, Scorpio can be self-destructive if they're too set on a dream or goal. To their advantage, Scorpio are often capable of recovering from bad decisions as they have regenerative abilities. Naturally stubborn, Scorpio are often the reason they have to recover from a situation in the first place. Along the way, Scorpio are extremely inventive and complex which can seem over-secretive or suspicious, but they're really just resourceful. Even though they can be short-tempered, Scorpio are very empathic and in tune with others. Passionate about life and determined to come out on top, Scorpio are one of the most successful signs when it comes to getting the job done.

Sagittarius
November 22 – December 21

We all want to know the meaning of life, but for Sagittarius, this truth seeking fuels their existence. Natural born philosophers, the Sagittarius are clear thinkers and often consider the whole picture. Being that they search for depth in life, Sagittarius commonly attract others who are spiritual and on a path of internal growth. While Sagittarius can become overly optimistic or exaggerative at times, their free-thinking is a great asset in what makes them who they are. It's important for their social growth and mental health that they are surrounded by people who won't misinterpret their blunt nature or lack of social etiquette. Sagittarius are known to speak their mind and can be impatient and argumentative though they prefer to avoid unnecessary conflict. Big on adventure, you're most likely to appreciate a Sagittarius if you embark their journey with them. While on the quest for knowledge and truth, a Sagittarius will quickly recognize someone who is eager to embark the excursion together.

Capricorn
December 22 – January 19

It's rare you'll ever have to question a Capricorn's work ethic. This sign in particular is all about determination. While the road to success doesn't always come easy to Capricorn, the victory is well deserved and may be accompanied by fame and fortune. In an effort to maintain their safe and steady route to the top, a Capricorn is quick to dismiss people who don't align with their ambitions. Socially, this can make it hard for Capricorn to maintain healthy and balanced relationships. Being that their element is Earth, Capricorn prefer to remain very grounded and occasionally need to surround themselves with people who are more "free spirited" to help them consider less meticulous options. Though the Capricorn is known for being casual in many areas of their life, that doesn't mean they don't take things seriously – this includes romantic relationships. If you feel a Capricorn puts work before relationships, all you have to do is let them know because they're just as dedicated to their home life (they might just need a friendly reminder). You can expect Capricorn to be cautious, but that's just their responsible nature and preference to play by the rules.

Aquarius
January 20 – February 18

Symbolized by the Water Bearer, Aquarius are beings of consciousness who carry the weight of the world. Interested in constantly helping people, the Aquarius focuses most of its energy on making the universe a better place. Known for being heavily intellectual, Aquarian ideas are often deeply thought out. Though they love sharing their ideas, Aquarius are easily frustrated and impatient with people who don't share their same perspective or understand. Aquarius are a fixed sign which means they may struggle to adapt in new situations, though they're very inventive at finding new solutions and approaches. Despite their love for helping others, Aquarius have a weird way of expressing their affections on a personal level. Additionally, their need to help everyone can be draining if they don't learn to set boundaries. Career wise, Aquarius excel in positions of servitude (example: psychology, law enforcement and education). Aquarians are happiest when they're doing humanitarian work and will connect with a large number of people along the way.

Pisces
February 19 – March 20

Pisces are the twelfth and final sign of the zodiac. Spiritual and very emotional, Pisces are known for their sensitive nature and psychic abilities. Spiritually evolved, Pisces have a difficult time distinguishing their own feelings from the energies surrounding them which can appear "emotionally unstable" to onlookers. Pisces are happiest when they're immersed in artistic endeavors and prefer to live in a fantasy world to avoid conflict/negativity. Pisces are very charitable and selfless which can make them fall victim to selfish energies; they are easily taken advantage of. As big dreamers, Pisces are deeply romantic and devoted lovers but are easily depressed when their efforts aren't reciprocated. While the Pisces is one of the most gentle and selfless signs, it can occasionally be to the point of impracticality. Due to the insight and advanced perspective they're gifted with, Pisces have a tendency to feel misunderstood and alone. Give Pisces a chance; their sincerity, sensitivity and creativity are a rare find.

Note from the Author

Remember that while it's not necessarily a spiritual practice, Astrology is a great tool to gain objective insight into your patterns and behaviors (in return, helping you to grow spiritually). Everyone possesses positive and negative qualities. By understanding what your traits are and where they originate from, you can begin making adjustments in your life so that things run smoother.

While this chapter only vaguely scratched the surface of Astrology, it should serve as a helpful guide towards better understanding your sun sign. When I first started reading into Astrology I was so overwhelmed with the amount of math and science involved. It was for that very reason I decided to keep this chapter as simple as possible. If you're interested in further exploring Astrology, I would encourage you to check out information on the Astrological Houses, Moon Signs and Ophiuchus (the 13th sign that was dropped from the Zodiac).

On the next few pages, I'm providing you some charts to compare the people you know with the qualities associated with their sign. Personally, I have a difficult time connecting with Astrology, though I do have a lot of fun reading into the signs and comparing people to the traits of their sign. Initially, I was hesitant about including this chapter, but spirit has reassured me that we all have something to learn from it. Even if you don't fit into your zodiac sign, there's something to gain from examining your life and seeing possibilities beyond your own experience and existence. I started keeping a log of each person I looked up and thought you might enjoy doing the same! I filled out the first profile using my information as an example. Interesting enough, despite my hesitations with astrology, I fit the Pisces sign to a tee!

THE DIVINITY DOCTRINE

Name Steven Binko   **Relation** Author
Birthday February 25th 1988   Sign Pisces
Ruling Planet(s) & Influence Neptune + Jupiter (co-ruler)
Illusion, dreams, spirituality, art, addiction, luck, inspiration and greater fortune.

- ☐ Cardinal   ☐ Fixed   ■ Mutable
- ☐ Air   ☐ Earth   ☐ Fire   ■ Water

About Very sensitive in nature, psychic abilities and led by emotions. Happy when involved with art. Sensitive nature occasionally taken advantage of. Deeply romantic. May feel misunderstood at times.

On a scale of 1 to 10, how does this person match their sign?

☐	☐	☐	☐	☐	☐	☐	☐	☐	■
1	2	3	4	5	6	7	8	9	10

Name   Relation

Birthday   Sign
Ruling Planet(s) & Influence

- ☐ Cardinal   ☐ Fixed   ☐ Mutable
- ☐ Air   ☐ Earth   ☐ Fire   ☐ Water

About

On a scale of 1 to 10, how does this person match their sign?

☐	☐	☐	☐	☐	☐	☐	☐	☐	☐
1	2	3	4	5	6	7	8	9	10

Name   **Relation**

Birthday   Sign

Ruling Planet(s) & Influence

☐ Cardinal   ☐ Fixed   ☐ Mutable
☐ Air   ☐ Earth   ☐ Fire   ☐ Water

About

On a scale of 1 to 10, how does this person match their sign?
☐   ☐   ☐   ☐   ☐   ☐   ☐   ☐   ☐   ☐
1   2   3   4   5   6   7   8   9   10

Name   **Relation**

Birthday   Sign

Ruling Planet(s) & Influence

☐ Cardinal   ☐ Fixed   ☐ Mutable
☐ Air   ☐ Earth   ☐ Fire   ☐ Water

About

On a scale of 1 to 10, how does this person match their sign?
☐   ☐   ☐   ☐   ☐   ☐   ☐   ☐   ☐   ☐
1   2   3   4   5   6   7   8   9   10

THE DIVINITY DOCTRINE

Name   **Relation**

Birthday   Sign

Ruling Planet(s) & Influence

☐ Cardinal   ☐ Fixed   ☐ Mutable
☐ Air   ☐ Earth   ☐ Fire   ☐ Water

About

On a scale of 1 to 10, how does this person match their sign?

☐ ☐ ☐ ☐ ☐ ☐ ☐ ☐ ☐ ☐
1 2 3 4 5 6 7 8 9 10

Name   **Relation**

Birthday   Sign

Ruling Planet(s) & Influence

☐ Cardinal   ☐ Fixed   ☐ Mutable
☐ Air   ☐ Earth   ☐ Fire   ☐ Water

About

On a scale of 1 to 10, how does this person match their sign?

☐ ☐ ☐ ☐ ☐ ☐ ☐ ☐ ☐ ☐
1 2 3 4 5 6 7 8 9 10

Name   **Relation**

Birthday   Sign

Ruling Planet(s) & Influence

☐ Cardinal   ☐ Fixed   ☐ Mutable
☐ Air   ☐ Earth   ☐ Fire   ☐ Water
About

On a scale of 1 to 10, how does this person match their sign?
☐   ☐   ☐   ☐   ☐   ☐   ☐   ☐   ☐   ☐
1   2   3   4   5   6   7   8   9   10

Name   **Relation**

Birthday   Sign

Ruling Planet(s) & Influence

☐ Cardinal   ☐ Fixed   ☐ Mutable
☐ Air   ☐ Earth   ☐ Fire   ☐ Water
About

On a scale of 1 to 10, how does this person match their sign?
☐   ☐   ☐   ☐   ☐   ☐   ☐   ☐   ☐   ☐
1   2   3   4   5   6   7   8   9   10

THE DIVINITY DOCTRINE

Name   **Relation**

Birthday   Sign

Ruling Planet(s) & Influence

☐ Cardinal   ☐ Fixed   ☐ Mutable
☐ Air   ☐ Earth   ☐ Fire   ☐ Water

About

On a scale of 1 to 10, how does this person match their sign?
☐   ☐   ☐   ☐   ☐   ☐   ☐   ☐   ☐   ☐
1   2   3   4   5   6   7   8   9   10

Name   **Relation**

Birthday   Sign

Ruling Planet(s) & Influence

☐ Cardinal   ☐ Fixed   ☐ Mutable
☐ Air   ☐ Earth   ☐ Fire   ☐ Water

About

On a scale of 1 to 10, how does this person match their sign?
☐   ☐   ☐   ☐   ☐   ☐   ☐   ☐   ☐   ☐
1   2   3   4   5   6   7   8   9   10

Chapter Six

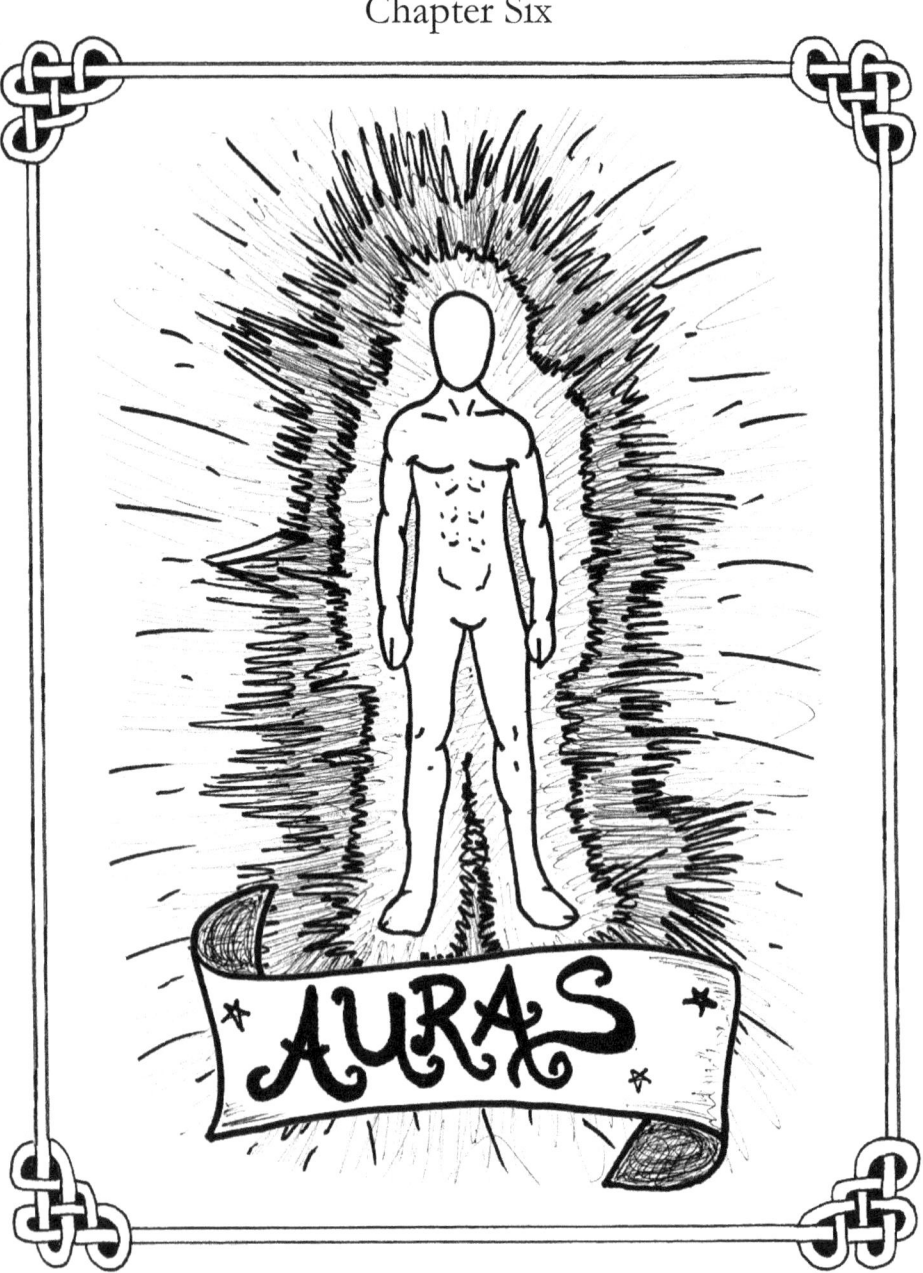

There is an "invisible" sphere of energy that surrounds and emanates from living things.

AURAS

Every living thing on the planet is surrounded by a sphere of energy known as an Aura. While it's generally accepted that an aura is invisible to the human eye, many people are capable of training themselves to see this energy field. If visible, an aura can take on many shapes, sizes, colors and opacities. The characteristics of an aura reflect the physical, emotional, mental and energy status of the living thing it surrounds. Like the synopsis on a book sleeve, the aura is a sneak peek into the core of a living thing; it doesn't tell the whole story, but we can get a general idea of its overall state of existence. Auras are not permanent and change with each internal shift of being. Just as each color in the visible color spectrum is defined by its individual wavelength and vibration, the vibrations emitted by a living thing translate into different aura colors.

Have you ever met someone and had a strange feeling they were trouble? That "vibe" is actually your body emotionally translating the aura emitted from that person. Often, maternal instincts are actually a direct result of unknowingly tapping into a child's aura. For mothers (having carried a baby inside of them), they are very familiar with their child's energy. Even when a child shows no visible symptoms of illness, a mother may have a sense of knowing in their gut that something isn't right.

The best way to begin reading a person's aura is to first identify with energy. A good exercise for this involves starting with your hands apart, visualizing energy emitted from your hands and slowly move your hands together until you feel energetic resistance. In doing this, you are able to identify how expansive your own energy field is at the present time. As your hands get closer, you may feel a push (like when you put two magnets against each other) or even feel a tingling in your fingertips. Once you've identified your own energy, begin noticing how you're physically affected when near someone else's energy field. A helpful suggestion is to keep a journal of what you sense when coming into contact with someone. Later, they might say or do something that reveals why you were able to pick up on a certain emotion.

Aura Cleansing

Throughout your day, you are constantly coming into contact with different energies and emotions. As you encounter these vibrations, your aura can get polluted. Your body is like an energy magnet; everywhere you go, you can absorb other people's energy. By learning to cleanse and protect yourself from other people's energy, you can retain a clearer, more authentic aura (as well as improve your chakra health).

The easiest way to protect your aura is to imagine surrounding yourself with a bubble made of white light; almost like a shield. By setting a daily intention, you're essentially helping to deflect anything negative. You are now able to select what you allow into your life. Some helpful ways to clear your aura include: meditation, smudging, Reiki, grounding exercises and crystal therapy. Simply connecting with nature (put your hands on a tree or your bare feet in the dirt while doing breathing exercises) is a great way to clear your auric field in a single session. Allow the earth to replenish you with pure energy and surround you with gold and white light from the earth's core.

Color Meanings

As a general guide, many of the basic aura colors can be associated with their chakra meanings. If a color is composed of two primary colors or has other color tones in it, combine both color meanings. Take for example a metallic blue. Simple blue is about communication and the metallic factor (silver) is about spirituality – combined, metallic blue means a person may communicate with the spirit world or be a speaker about something spiritual.

Red: *One of the most symbolically diverse colors, red symbolizes passion in every sense of the word. A pure red is often associated with love, intense sexuality, and courage. If a red is polluted (mud like), this can signify a more disconnected and materialistic person.*

Orange: *Alone, this color represents empathic nature. Composed of red and yellow, orange as a whole represents creativity and high energy in social settings (adventurous, outgoing, and able to connect with people).*

Yellow: *People with simple yellow auras are full of life. Able to take creative approaches to challenges, yellow is a color of intellectuality. People with a lot of yellow in their aura have a tendency to ask a lot of questions and are constantly striving to better understand life.*

Green: *Alone, green represents a connection with nature and balance. People with green in their auras are often holistic healers. Composed of yellow and blue, green is a balance between creativity and practicality.*

Blue: *Most often, blue auras are seen on public speakers and officials who mediate or keep peace. Blue is a color of communication and represents emotional balance. People who channel or who have telepathic abilities often emit blue as it's a high-frequency color.*

Purple: *This is a very common color for people who are psychic, artistic, philosophical and in tune with the universe. Many times, people with purple auras are also unconventional and free spirited.*

Brown: *When mixed with a color, brown represents disconnect from the actual colors meaning or a blockage in that area of someone's life. Brown alone signifies fear, confusion, insecurity and a focus on material belongings.*

Black: *Seeing a person surrounded by a black aura is a rare occurrence. Generally speaking, black shows up as spots in the aura field. When this happens, it may represent signs of major illness (likely in the area you see the spots) or extreme negativity and deep hatred.*

White: *There are few reports of people seeing an entirely white aura surrounding someone (unless they're close to dying). When mixed with another color to make it appear faded, this represents purity in nature regarding the secondary color. As an example, while red represents passion, pink (red and white) represents a more pure intention in love (tender and sensitive). Spots, sparkles, or a haze of white in a person's aura may indicate an angelic presence or pregnancy.*

Silver/Gold: *Alone, silver or gold suggests angelic presence, a strong connection with the divine, protection and enlightenment. When mixed with another color to make metallic tones, this represents sensitivity and intuitive perspective regarding what the initial color symbolizes.*

Chapter Seven

Each month of the year is associated with a special stone. What's your stone and the story behind it?

BIRTHSTONES

Dating back as far as biblical times, stones have played a very symbolic role in both history and mythology. In Exodus, a breastplate was made by Moses (1250 BC) for Aaron - High Priest of the Hebrews. Designed with 12 different stones, historians later associated each stone with a specific month out of the year. In more recent years, the jewelry industry modified the stone charts to better supply customer demands with more elegant looking gemstones. Though cultural interpretations and adaptations vary, this chapter outlines the most widely used stone selections prior to the newly adapted standardized lists.

MONTH	STONE	STONE PROPERTIES
January	Garnet	Extracts negative energy, enhances creativity and productivity, attracts love, restores confidence and sharpens perception. Aids in chakra health.
February	Amethyst	Carries a high vibration that is useful in meditation or to achieve tranquility. Improves psychic intuition by assisting the third eye which can also help in connecting with Angels & Guides.
March	Aquamarine	Provides a shield for your aura and spiritual body. Aids in connecting with your higher self. Brings out confidence and courage. Is believed to be a stone of eternal youth.
April	Diamond	Strengthens willpower and control over your physical desires by uniting the body with the mind. Enhances abundance and trust as well as the powers of other crystals and stones.
May	Emerald	Balances emotional chaos. Encourages you to serve more and evaluate the spiritual areas of your life. Intensifies chakra energies, protects against temptation and brings prosperity.

Month	Stone	Properties
June	Pearl	Calming, attracts purity and promotes integrity. Aids in connecting with divine or feminine energies which is also believed to improve fertility. Signifies faith and provides truth.
July	Ruby	Opens your heart to unconditional love. Protects that which you have strong connections with. Reduces fear and repressed emotions. Brings happiness and loyalty.
August	Peridot	Assists in rebirth. Brings abundance and enhances harmony between people. Aids in finding lost objects and strengthens psychic abilities. Can provide emotional/spiritual protection.
September	Sapphire	Increases concentration and stimulates psychic awareness. Brings spiritual "knowing" which can reduce doubt and anxiety. Helps to connect with your higher self.
October	Opal	Assists in adapting to 3D planetary changes and spiritual shifts. Works with emotions and lightens your aura. Increases the speed of manifestation (both positive and negative).
November	Topaz	Promotes creativity and restores confidence. Assists in astral projection and detoxification. Attracts good people and success in business. Replaces negativity with joy.
December	Turquoise	Enables meditation and brings peace of mind while aligning the chakras. Known to assist in telepathy. Is also a serious filter for negative energies.

Everyone can benefit from the individual properties associated with the different birthstones regardless of what their assigned stone is. You can even combine different stones to promote overall chakra health or treat multiple issues at the same time.

NOTES

Chapter Eight

Candles are more powerful than you think.
Learn how and when to use them.

CANDLES

Whether you're looking to set the mood for a romantic dinner or casting a spell, candles are great compliment to any occasion. Historically, candles have played a part in traditions worldwide since before Christ. Considering bees were respected as messengers of the Gods in ancient Egypt, candles were initially made of beeswax and were believed to hold magical powers. In later years, Christianity adapted the use of candles in many of its traditions. To this day, beeswax candles are still used in Christian churches. Many cultures even treat the actual flame of a candle as though it represents life. Religion aside, candles are a great tool in promoting spiritual development or simply providing light when the power goes out!

Like any metaphysical tool, understanding its significance plays a crucial part in utilizing it effectively. Many times, it is the intention we establish when using a spiritual tool that determines its value. A great example of this is the religious cross. While two pieces of wood glued together have no special powers on their own, it's when we exude energy into the significance we give them that their "power" is established. As with most things in life, we create our reality through the law of attraction and that which we find true to ourselves. When you're able to fully understand why a particular candle has been used for thousands of years, it will help your conscience affirm and project its intended energy. Furthermore, science has shown that the simple atmosphere created by a lit candle is powerful enough to induce moments of euphoria or reflection as the mind calms.

For whatever reason you've stumbled upon this chapter, the following information should prove useful in harnessing a candle's full potential.

OCCASIONS CANDLES ARE COMMONLY USED

Baptism, wedding, birthday, funeral, holidays, spells, tributes, prayer, romantic occasions, power outages, to provide heat, aromatherapy, protection, chakra balancing, dining, decoration, time keeping, etc.

Candle Colors & Uses

Utilizing different candle colors is a great way to focus certain energies towards the purpose you desire. When utilizing colored candles, it is generally recommended that they are solid in color all the way through. Scientifically, each hue in the visible color spectrum carries its own frequency – this is how our eye distinguishes one color from the next. That in mind, consider the power that simply illuminating a color has on the universe. Each time you light a candle, you're igniting energy from the flame as well as radiating vibrations of color wavelengths (energy) from the colored wax. It's incredible how powerful a single candle is!

Red: *Red candles should only be burned when in a positive state of mind. Commonly used to attract love, sex, and courage, it's a color that deals with matters of pleasure and strength. That being said, red is a low vibration color which can cause unintentional chaos and damage. Be sure that when attempting to attract love that your intentions don't stem from lust. When looking for courage or strength, be sure that you're not coming from rage or domination. Your true intentions will manifest when burning a red candle. Red candles can be used to treat the root chakra.*

Orange: *When dealing with social matters, Orange is a very effective candle color. Often used when searching for self-esteem, friendship, and bringing people together, orange is a color that attracts harmony into situations dealing with people's personalities. This can be a great tool when requiring independence or embarking on creative endeavors. Orange candles can be used to treat the sacral chakra.*

Yellow: *Of all the colors, Yellow is the most effective for influencing or stimulating the mind. Aiding in concentration, memory, and logic, yellow candles are especially useful when looking to gain other people's confidence regarding creative or business matters. Second to green, it can also be great for attracting luck or success through intelligence. Yellow can be used to treat the solar plexus chakra.*

Green: *Commonly used to attract money, luck and deal with jealousy, it should be noted that green is also a powerful healer. Invoking powers from the earth and empathy for others, Green has a heavy influence on emotional matters. Green can be used to treat the heart chakra.*

Blue: *Blue candles are an amazing tool when looking to expand your possibilities. A color of peace and knowledge, blue candles are most effective when ethics are in question or security is at stake. If you're in a situation that requires judgment (example: court, work, etc.), blue is excellent at revealing the truth and works in the favor of honor. If you're experiencing a crisis, blue is also helpful in bringing peace and calm. Blue candles can be used to treat the throat chakra.*

Purple: *On a spiritual level, purple candles are invaluable. They're great for increasing psychic insight, enhancing intuition, aiding in mediation, easing astral travel/helping to access higher dimensions, and tapping into divine wisdom. The power of purple also protects against evil and nightmares. Allowing you to see what you truly long for and helping to let go of the past, purple goes beyond your material yearnings and fulfills your soul-deep desires. Many times, purple candles are lit in memoriam of a loved one that has died. Purple candles can be used to treat the throat and crown chakras.*

Pink: *Just as it appears, pink is a gentle color that deals with light-hearted matters. Pink candles are great when you're looking to win someone's affection or friendship. In family situations, it's great for rekindling and easing hurt feelings.*

White: *Offering protection and aiding in efforts to connect with angels or guides, white is a color that brings purity. White candles are most commonly used in ceremonies or celebrations of new beginnings like birth and marriage. White is known to cleanse and provide protection against negativity or bad health. If you're looking for clear vision on a situation, white is also a great candle to "clean the slate" and start new.*

Black: *The color black is made up of all the hues in the visible color spectrum (it can also be complete absence of light). When ignited in the form of a candle, the vibration from this powerful collection of colors can break spells, banish evil, end bad relationships and define both physical and spiritual boundaries. It's a great tool for reducing negativity.*

Brown: *Brown is an earth tone that invokes powers from the planet while providing grounding, a foundation and balance. It can be used to help find lost things and to deal with other practical matters. Brown is also helpful when dealing with pets, children and the elderly.*

Gray/Silver: *Colors for divination and spiritual awakening, gray and silver are helpful with meditation, clairvoyance, astral projection, and telepathy. They may be used to clear negativity.*

Gold: *Used on its own or hand in hand with green, gold candles are a great color for financial success. In the work place, gold is helpful in attaining employment or receiving recognition. Lastly, gold can be used with any other color to speed up or provide more abundant results.*

Reinforce your intentions

When lighting a candle, there are two ways that you can reinforce your intentions. Write what you desire on a piece of paper. After you've lit the candle, fold the paper and ignite it with the flame. As the ashes fall into the wax, the energy of what you wrote on the paper will continue to spread as the candle continues to burn. An alternate method is carving your desire into the side of the candle's wax.

Note from the author

Culturally, there are many variations in the powers believed to be associated with different color candles. The meanings and uses I provided are based solely on my interpretation of what spirit tells me. On a human level, I've established negative connotations with certain color candles which significantly affects which colors I choose to use. As I mentioned earlier, the energetic capabilities are often dependent on the energy you exude. If you feel any resistance against using a certain color, don't use it - you would be putting out your fearful and negative energy which could completely counteract your intended purpose. As you read the explanations I provided, see which you connect with on a soul level and go from there. Many times, I will even use a clear or white candle after I've implanted my energetic blueprint and intentions. If you choose to go that route, you may also visualize coloring the white candle with energy from the chakra of the corresponding color. Many people enjoy accompanying their candle rituals with fragrances, herbs, gems, oils, or even flowers to enhance their power.

NOTES

Chapter Nine

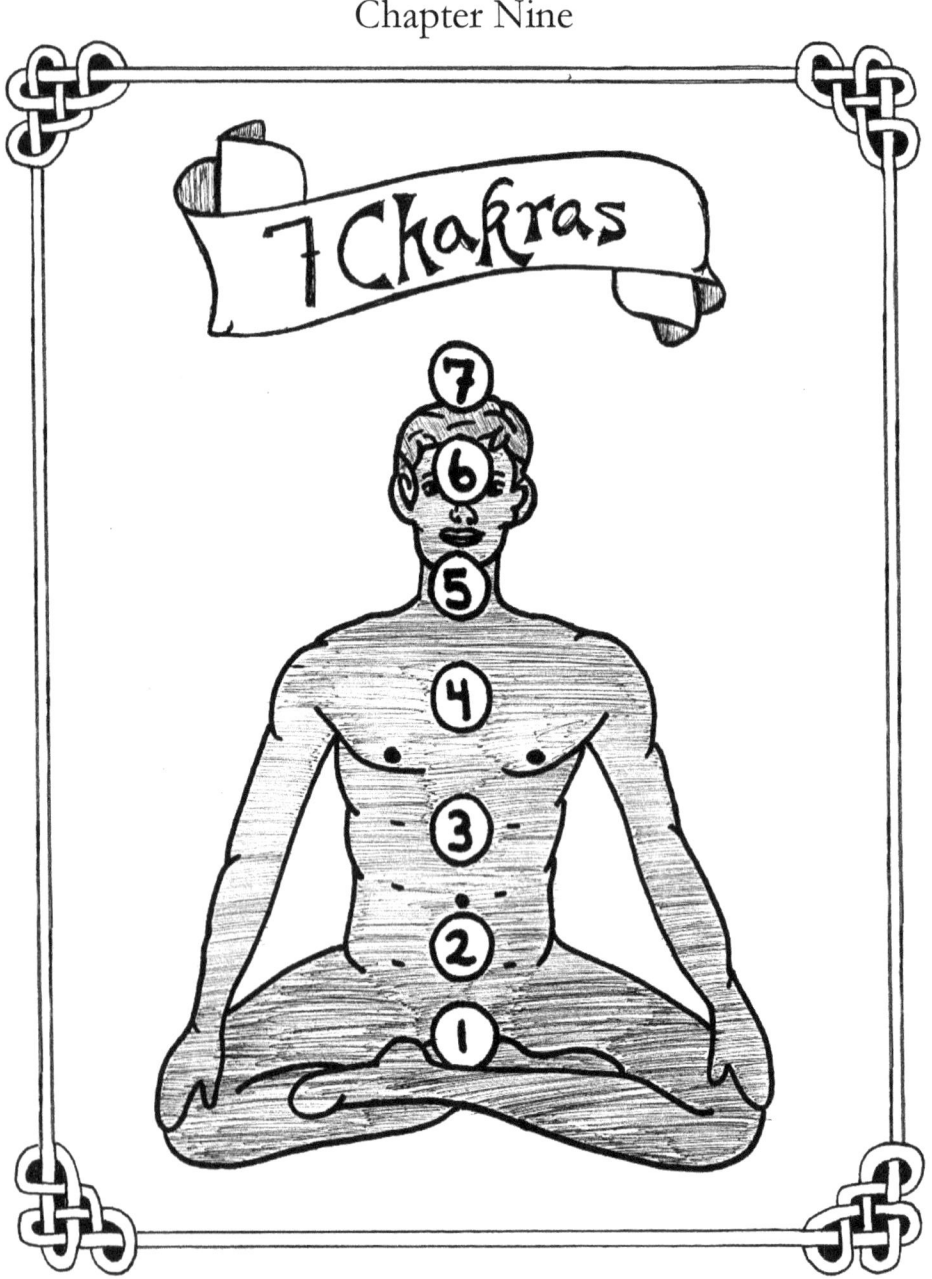

The seven centers of spiritual power in the human body.

CHAKRAS

In each of our bodies there is a series of energy centers called chakras. Each of the seven major chakras relate to a unique aspect of our being. It's important to clear these chakras regularly to perform at your highest potential as a blockage in a chakra's energy cycle can result in physical, mental, emotional, or spiritual issues and disorders.

Overview

1. Root Chakra : Red
    - Located at the base of the spine by the genitals and tailbone
    - Deals with survival, self-sufficiency, stability and being grounded.

2. Sacral Chakra : Orange
    - Located in the lower abdomen below the belly button.
    - Deals with well-being, sexuality, healing and emotional identity.

3. Solar Plexus Chakra : Yellow
    - Located in the upper abdomen by the stomach area.
    - Deals with self-worth/confidence, stamina and ego.

4. Heart Chakra : Green
    - Located at the center of the chest just above the heart.
    - Deals with unconditional love, joy, compassion and inner peace.

5. Throat Chakra : Blue
    - Located in the throat.
    - Deals with communication, truthfulness and judgment.

6. Third Eye / Brow Chakra : Indigo
    - Located at the center of the forehead between the eyes
    - Deals with intuition, imagination, wisdom and perception.

7. Crown Chakra : Violet
    - Located at the very top of the head / just above head.
    - Deals with divine purpose, spiritual consciousness and intuition.

Chakra Colors & Science

The visible light spectrum can be broken down into 7 different colors: Red, Orange, Yellow, Green, Blue, Indigo, and Violet. Scientifically speaking, each of these colors has its own vibration. The molecular composition and chemical activity of a color determines the speed of light that's returned to the eye which translates to the color that we see. Each color has its own frequency due to its unique wavelengths. Red has the longest wavelength and slowest vibration, whereas Violet has the shortest wavelength and fastest vibration. This is why we respond differently both physically and emotionally to different colors For example, red feels warm because of the slow vibration and blue feels cold because of the fast vibration. By managing these frequencies, you can directly improve your physical and spiritual health.

Chakra Health

Because each chakra resonates with a different color, the colors that you surround yourself with can have a profound effect on the health and functionality of each chakra. Think of it this way: If your favorite color is blue and you continually wear blue clothing, you're surrounding your body with the vibration that color carries. It's basic science. This is why it's important we're exposed to the sun (which carries a variety of light and color vibrations). The light vibration contributes energy and life to everything ranging from humans to plants. So, if you continually overexpose a chakra to a certain color it can over-boost that area causing an overload of energy. On the other hand, if you're not exposed to enough of a certain color, your chakra may develop a deficiency.

By ingesting foods with colors that coordinate with the chakra that needs charging, you are capable of directly influencing your physical, mental and spiritual well-being. The way you paint your house, the color of the clothing you wear, and even the color of your car has a significant influence on your overall health. Some very useful tools you can use to balance, activate and charge your chakras include: light therapy, crystals *(see chapter 10)*, mediation to visualize colors surrounding each chakra, music vibration therapy, yoga, and seeing an energy practitioner.

So, what causes blockages in the first place? While the events in your day-to-day life can pollute your chakras, events and emotions buried in your subconscious for too long can manifest and spread like a virus. Traumatic events, restrictive belief systems, tainted relationships or even emotions from abandonment can cause a chakra to completely shut down. Even past-life situations and karmic imbalance can influence your present life chakra health. Like most illnesses, if left un-treated, the problem generally grows and requires more time and effort to heal. From a psychological or medical standpoint, these life experience scenarios cause the body to harbor tension, feelings of guilt and suppressed emotions.

Over the course of your life, your experiences and social conditioning form your beliefs and perceptions. The challenge is to recognize the disharmony within yourself and explore the possible causes. As you begin to accept and process these repressed issues, you will find yourself more capable of dealing directly with present life situations and stressors. Until you release what you're holding on to, you're limited from receiving anything new (good or bad). While it can be difficult to forgive and release past situations, holding onto them only hurts you. Allow your mind, body and spirit to rejuvenate itself. Along the way, the most important thing is to allow yourself the necessary time to heal without putting pressure on yourself in the process. Try not to "polish" off something ugly and hold onto it. Rather, throw it away to make room for something new and improved. The choice is yours – you will ultimately create and be responsible for your present reality.

Medically, there is a great amount of scientific evidence that stress can cause a wide variety of negative side effects on the body. When a chakra is out of balance, it can put stress on the human body; in return, manifesting in a variety of ways. Through opening, activating, charging, balancing, and clearing your chakras on a regular basis, you can live a healthier and more balanced life.

Unresolved issues aside, if a chakra is simply over-exposed or under-exposed to particular types of energy (color vibration or negative energy), it can easily make an individual feel overwhelmed and over-sensitive. These imbalances can manifest themselves in a variety of physical and mental side-effects.

With many of the changes occurring on a planetary level (such as the Ascension), it is more important than ever to acknowledge your chakra health. If you've found yourself more irritable than usual, this could be a result of your astral body and chakras struggling to adjust to the change in frequency that comes with the shifts happening. If you imagined your chakra's like "gears", imagine a "bolt" that's jamming them up. If you haven't tuned into your chakra health for a long time, it's also possible they just need a little "oil" to reduce the friction from sitting still so long. Sometimes a little help is all that's needed for a well-oiled machine to run smoothly.

You may consider reading the "grounding" chapter for a chakra grounding exercise called the "Chakra Elevator Technique".

<u>Identifying Issues</u>

Deficiency Characteristics : You might find yourself getting colds on a frequent basis (feeling sick). When it comes to making decisions, you're not capable of thinking properly and are affected by feelings of paranoia, self-consciousness and indecisiveness. Your mentality shifts to blaming others often as a result of fear that you'll be rejected. Some people even suffer with self-discipline - often challenged with increased attraction to stimulants to get that "boost".

Energetic Overload Symptoms : If you're acting out of character and seem to be more dominating, manipulative, deceitful or stubborn, you could have excessive amounts of energy built up. If over-exposed for extended amounts of time, a person may become power hungry, competitive and possessive. Occasionally, you're using tools like sex and money to get what you want (operating from low vibration). In this scenario, it's not uncommon to find attraction to sedatives to calm down the over active mind and body.

Physical Symptoms of Imbalance : When your body begins to feel more anxious, sad or depressed than usual, it manifests physically. Some symptoms include respiratory issues and high blood pressure. Stomach and digestive problems such as ulcers and diarrhea can develop. There is a risk of insomnia or fatigue despite regular sleep patterns as well.

NOTES

Chapter Ten

Like people, crystals and stones also have their own personalities and strengths.

CRYSTALS & STONES

Aesthetically speaking, crystals and stones are some of the most beautiful gifts from nature. While some crystals and stones can take just minutes to form, others may take centuries. From a metaphysical perspective however, these treasures have more to offer than just their beauty. Like people, each crystal and stone has its own personality and strength. The use of stones and crystals throughout history is well documented and appears in almost every culture across the world. Discovered in the ruins of Babylon, the tombs of ancient Egyptian rulers, mentioned throughout the Bible and appearing in Chinese medicine for over 5000 years, even the oldest civilizations were aware of their metaphysical properties.

In this chapter, crystals and stones will occasionally be referred to as rocks. Although I'll be doing this to avoid sounding repetitive, please note that while all crystals and stones are technically rocks, not all rocks are crystals – but that's a chapter for another time!

Charging & Cleansing

Before integrating their energies into your life, it's important to cleanse your rock. The most common way to do this involves holding the rock in your hand, setting your intentions (also called "dedicating") and removing negativity through visualization. Alternatively, some people prefer to use sage, set the rock in brown rice or soak it in salt water. Personally, I prefer to bury my rocks in the dirt - allowing the earth soak out unnatural energies. It should be noted that while salt water can be highly effective, the composition of the rock may not take well to the salt – causing irreversible physical/aesthetic damage.

Occasionally, rocks require a recharge. This can be done by visualization, though if you're feeling negative it's recommended you set them in the sunlight to absorb the sun's life-force rays/energy instead. If you choose to cleanse your stone in the ocean (salt water) on a sunny day, you are actually cleansing AND charging your rock at the same time!

Practical Uses

Due to the stable and measurable frequency of Quartz, for example, many modern technologies like clocks, computers and radios were once built with crystals. To this day, some devices are still manufactured with them. We have infinite power within ourselves, but each rock has defining energies that can aid us in our day-to-day lives. These energies can be helpful with: chakra balancing, providing safety and protection, fixing mechanical problems, dowsing with pendulums *(see chapter 11)*, meditation, and improving your health.

Chakra Balancing: *If a particular Chakra isn't functioning normally due to a lack of energy (or from too much energy), rocks are a great way to restore balance. The easiest and most time effective way to treat your Chakra is by carrying the corresponding rock in your pocket throughout the day or by wearing it as jewelry. If you're able to set aside 10-15 minutes, simply placing the rock on your body (over the Chakra) is just as effective. A fun method involves placing corresponding rocks under your mattress in the order of the seven Chakras – this way, you're recharging as you sleep. People who utilize this method are known to achieve a full nights rest in a shorter amount of time as the body receives the energy it needs faster than usual. Lastly, some people place rocks in or near the water they drink to raise the water's vibration. Should you choose to do this, know your rock's chemical composition to avoid contamination.*

Safety & Protection: *Many people place protection rocks in their cars on the dashboard, in the glove compartment, on a keychain or hang it on their rear-view mirror. Another common practice is placing protective rocks at the entrance of a home and on the nightstand next to a bed. While women commonly wear crystals and stones, many times they unknowingly reap the benefits of protective rocks. It is important to note that while different rocks are great for providing safety and protection, many of them also amplify and manifest thoughts and emotions. That being said, it is recommended you wear a rock only when in a positive state of mind (not fear based). If you incorporate rocks into your daily routine, it will be more beneficial than consciously putting one on because you have a bad feeling; provide yourself protection on an ongoing basis. Rocks can be a powerful protective tool, but the key to maximum utilization is understanding how and when to use them. Have faith and avoid thoughts that resist your rocks intended purpose.*

Meditation: *During a meditation, sit on the floor or bed. Place a variety of rocks in a circle around you to amplify the energy you draw in and put out. If you're meditating with a specific purpose, find the rock that correlates with the reason for your session and hold it in your hands. You may also close your eyes and hold it to your heart. Physically you may feel like you're holding onto something external/separate from your body, but you're actually interacting with the rock on a higher frequency energetically. By consciously making the decision to connect with the crystal or stone energy, you're helping to create energetic balance within your body – returning your body to a state of well-being.*

Finding Rocks

Finding rocks in your back yard isn't impossible, but finding the ones you're looking for is a lot harder. There are a few great resources to consider utilizing when looking to attain a specific stone. Many cities have metaphysical stores and rock shops which generally offer a wide variety of crystals, stones and gems. In these storefronts you can also find different variations of the same rock – raw and clustered, tumbled and polished or even carved into specific shapes. If you're looking for a unique way to hunt for rocks, mining (depending on your location) can be done for a nominal cost. Lastly, if you're looking for a rare rock, shopping online can prove to be very helpful and convenient. If you choose to utilize internet shopping, be cautious of the vendor you're purchasing through to ensure you're getting an authentic rock.

Crystal & Stone Properties

The following chart outlines the most popular crystals and stones used within the metaphysical community. Keep in mind this is not a complete guide. If you're interested in exploring which rock is your birthstone, reference chapter seven.

(chart begins on next page)

ROCK	METAPHYSICAL PROPERTIES
Agate	The rock of strength and courage. Also known to aid with expanding your perception. Can be used for grounding and to balance your 5th Chakra.
Amazonite	Gets your mind and body to work together. Calms nervousness by bringing joy and clarity. Can be used to balance the 5th Chakra.
Amethyst	Carries a high vibration that is useful in meditation or to achieve tranquility. Improves psychic intuition by assisting the third eye which can also help in connecting with Angels & Guides. Can be used to balance the 7th Chakra.
Aquamarine	Provides a shield for your aura and spiritual body. Aids in connecting with your higher self. Brings out confidence and courage. Is believed to be a stone of eternal youth. Balances the 5th Chakra.
Aventurine	Strengthens leadership and motivational skills. Promotes independence and prosperity. Relieves anger and fear. Can be used to treat the 4th Chakra.
Azurite	Awakens spiritual and personal transformation. Enhances creativity and self-confidence with social situations. Can be used to balance the 6th Chakra.
Bloodstone	Holds strong healing powers that banish negativity. A stone of renewal. Dispels confusion and provides wisdom. Balances the 1st and 4th Chakras.
Calcite	Connects your inner self with the environment and helps you to tune into nature frequencies. Can be used to remember astral travel experiences and creates a harmonic balance between Chakras.
Carnelian	Provides grounding with thoughts – allowing for more analytical yet creative thinking and improved memory. Gives courage and encourages sexuality. This rock can be used to cleanse other stones as well as balance the 2nd Chakra.
Chrysoprase	Brings new clarity to problems and awakens hidden talents. Balances attitudes and the 4th Chakra.
Citrine	Energizes. Helps to overcome depression by raising self-esteem. Attracts and maintains abundance. Can be used to balance the 3rd Chakra.

Diamond	Strengthens willpower and control over your physical desires by uniting the body with the mind. Enhances abundance and trust as well as the powers of other crystals and stones. Can be used to balance the 7th Chakra.
Emerald	Balances emotional chaos. Encourages you to serve more and evaluate the spiritual areas of your life. Intensifies chakra energies, protects against temptation and brings prosperity. Can be used to balance the 4th Chakra.
Fluorite	Overcomes chaos by improving coordination, providing protection, grounding and stability. Removes negativity, purifies and balances Chakras.
Garnet	Extracts negative energy, enhances creativity and productivity, attracts love, restores confidence and sharpens perception. Balances the 1st Chakra.
Hematite	Enhances willpower. Strengthens and energizes physical and soul bodies. Provides grounding. Aids in legal situations and helps to overcome stress. Drives away negativity (protective). Can be used to help balance the 1st Chakra.
Howlite	Aids with communication and self-expression to help reduce stress and pain that has manifested from thoughts. Promotes patience and better judgment. Can be used to balance the 5th Chakra.
Jade	Increases love, attracts good luck and friendship. Balances emotions and encourages wisdom. Promotes self-sufficiency. Stimulates ideas and helps to remember and understand dreams. Can be used for protection or to balance the 4th Chakra.
Jasper	Provides grounding for the physical body and balances all Chakras. Generally used to accompany other stones.
Kyanite	Great for meditation and getting in touch you're your higher self. Helps with self-expression and communication. Aligns the Chakras.
Lapis	Expands consciousness and intelligence. Known to enhance dreams (makes them more vivid) and awakens psychic intuition. Balances the 6th Chakra.

Malachite	Promotes spiritual growth as a whole. Clears the subconscious to promote change and alleviate shyness. Activates all Chakras and balances the 4th.
Moonstone	Stimulates confidence and heals emotions. Encourages lucid dreaming, intuitiveness and perception. Balances the 4th Chakra.
Obsidian	Protects against negative energy. Grounding and helps to clear subconscious blocks. Can be used to balance the 1st Chakra.
Onyx	Integrates duality. Teaches self-control. Promotes stamina and alleviates fear. Attracts happiness and good fortune. Creates harmonious flow in Chakras.
Opal	Assists in adapting to 3D planetary changes and spiritual shifts. Works with emotions and lightens your aura. Increases the speed of manifestation (both positive and negative). Various opal colors treat different Chakras, but primarily the 4th.
Pearl	Calming, attracts purity and promotes integrity. Aids in connecting with divine or feminine energies which is also believed to improve fertility. Signifies faith and provides truth. Works best without other rocks to create chakra balance.
Peridot	Assists in rebirth. Brings abundance and enhances harmony between people. Aids in finding lost objects and strengthens psychic abilities. Can provide emotional/spiritual protection. Used to balance the 4th Chakra.
Pyrite (Fool's Gold)	Inspires a positive attitude, greater understanding and alleviates despair. Improves memory and aids in matters of intelligence. Balances 1st Chakra.
Quartz (clear)	The most powerful healer and energy stone. Receives, stores, amplifies and transmits energy and thoughts. Aids in communication between the dimensions. Great for meditation and ridding negativity. Harmonizes all Chakras.
Quartz (rose)	Attracts unconditional love. Clears jealousy, guilt and anger. Encourages compassion, forgiveness and restores trust. Deals with matters of the heart. Can be used to balance the 4th Chakra.

Quartz (smoky)	Releases energetic blocks through grounding and protection. Dispels negativity. Can be used to balance the 1st Chakra.
Rhodonite	Maximizes your potential by raising your self-esteem and eliminating anxiety. Can be used to balance the 1st and 4th Chakras.
Ruby	Opens your heart to unconditional love. Protects that which you have strong connections with. Reduces fear and repressed emotions. Brings happiness and loyalty. Balances the 1st Chakra.
Sapphire	Increases concentration and stimulates psychic awareness. Brings spiritual "knowing" which can reduce doubt and anxiety. Helps to connect with your higher self. Primarily used to balance the 5th Chakra, but also effective with the 6th and 7th.
Selenite	Aids in connecting with your higher self. Helps with tuning into higher frequencies (contacting angels and guides). Balances 6th and 7th Chakras.
Sodalite	Heals the mind. Brings about clarity and truth. Enhances communication and the ability to express yourself. Balances the 6th Chakra.
Sunstone	Removes negativity. Grounds the 1st Chakra.
Tiger Eye	Stimulates Kundalini Rising (the coiled serpent at the base of the spine releases and travels up your Chakras leading to a spiritual awakening). Promotes clarity and optimism. Helps with overcoming stubbornness. Balances the 2nd and 3rd Chakras.
Topaz	Promotes creativity and restores confidence. Assists in astral projection and detoxification. Attracts good people and success in business. Replaces negativity with joy. Balances the 2nd and 3rd Chakras.
Tourmaline	A stone of protection. Prevents fears and fights off negativity. Pulls toxicity from the Chakras.
Turquoise	Enables meditation and brings peace of mind while aligning the chakras. Known to assist in telepathy. Is also a serious filter for negative energies. Can be used to balance the 5th Chakra.
Unakite	Facilitates the birthing process. Can be used to balance the 4th Chakra.

Exercises

The following includes a list of various exercises and worksheets so that you can track your experience with different crystals and stones.

The Placebo Challenge: *This exercise is especially effective with skeptics who suggest people only see the benefits they're looking for from a rock. The Placebo Effect suggests that people are influenced by their thoughts and expectations as opposed to reaping real physical, mental or spiritual benefits. To challenge this theory, carry your rock with you over the course of a month before looking up its metaphysical qualities. Using the provided journal, document any changes or unusual situations that occur over the course of that time. After you've completed the month, look up your stone and review its properties. Does it reflect the changes you experienced while carrying the stone with you?*

Overnight Charge: *As mentioned earlier in this chapter, a method of charging your chakras involves placing corresponding rocks under your mattress in the order of the seven Chakras – this way, you're recharging as you sleep. People who utilize this method are known to achieve a full nights rest in a shorter amount of time as the body receives the energy it needs faster than usual. You're being provided a sleep journal to track your energy levels and sleep times.*

Gracious Giver: *Carry a small pouch of stones or crystals with you on a daily basis. Once you feel you've reaped the benefits of a particular rock, either leave it behind for a stranger to find or hand it to someone and explain its purpose. Should you choose to leave your rock somewhere for someone to find, visualize infusing it with positivity and unconditional love. Perhaps a child will discover this new treasure or an adult who is having a bad day will see something pretty when everything in their life feels ugly. If you consciously hand your rock off to someone else, you don't have to explain the metaphysical characteristics if it makes you nervous. Instead, simply tell them it's brought you good luck and that you just wanted to pass it on! It should be noted that on occasion, after a rock has fulfilled its purpose, it will randomly become "lost". While it can be sad to lose an object of beauty, appreciate the beauty in knowing it journeyed into the hands of someone deserving. The gracious giver exercise simply allows you to part with your rock on your own terms.*

THE PLACEBO CHALLENGE - TEST #1

START DATE	ROCK	END DATE

WEEK 1

WEEK 2

WEEK 3

WEEK 4

CONCLUSION

THE PLACEBO CHALLENGE - TEST #2

START DATE	ROCK	END DATE

WEEK 1

WEEK 2

WEEK 3

WEEK 4

CONCLUSION

THE PLACEBO CHALLENGE - TEST #3

START DATE	ROCK	END DATE

WEEK 1	

WEEK 2	

WEEK 3	

WEEK 4	

CONCLUSION	

THE PLACEBO CHALLENGE - TEST #4

START DATE	ROCK	END DATE

WEEK 1	

WEEK 2	

WEEK 3	

WEEK 4	

CONCLUSION	

THE PLACEBO CHALLENGE - TEST #5

START DATE	ROCK	END DATE

WEEK 1

WEEK 2

WEEK 3

WEEK 4

CONCLUSION

THE PLACEBO CHALLENGE - TEST #6

START DATE	ROCK	END DATE

WEEK 1

WEEK 2

WEEK 3

WEEK 4

CONCLUSION

OVERNIGHT CHARGE – JOURNAL ENTRY #1

DATE	BED TIME	WAKE TIME	TOTAL TIME

DID YOU WAKE UP EARLIER THAN YOU INTENDED? ☐ YES ☐ NO

HOW RESTED ARE YOU ON A SCALE OF 1 to 10?

☐ 1 ☐ 2 ☐ 3 ☐ 4 ☐ 5 ☐ 6 ☐ 7 ☐ 8 ☐ 9 ☐ 10

NOTES:

OVERNIGHT CHARGE – JOURNAL ENTRY #2

DATE	BED TIME	WAKE TIME	TOTAL TIME

DID YOU WAKE UP EARLIER THAN YOU INTENDED? ☐ YES ☐ NO

HOW RESTED ARE YOU ON A SCALE OF 1 to 10?

☐ 1 ☐ 2 ☐ 3 ☐ 4 ☐ 5 ☐ 6 ☐ 7 ☐ 8 ☐ 9 ☐ 10

NOTES:

OVERNIGHT CHARGE – JOURNAL ENTRY #3

DATE	BED TIME	WAKE TIME	TOTAL TIME

DID YOU WAKE UP EARLIER THAN YOU INTENDED? ☐ YES ☐ NO

HOW RESTED ARE YOU ON A SCALE OF 1 to 10?

☐ 1 ☐ 2 ☐ 3 ☐ 4 ☐ 5 ☐ 6 ☐ 7 ☐ 8 ☐ 9 ☐ 10

NOTES:

OVERNIGHT CHARGE – JOURNAL ENTRY #4

DATE	BED TIME	WAKE TIME	TOTAL TIME

DID YOU WAKE UP EARLIER THAN YOU INTENDED? ☐ YES ☐ NO

HOW RESTED ARE YOU ON A SCALE OF 1 to 10?

☐ 1 ☐ 2 ☐ 3 ☐ 4 ☐ 5 ☐ 6 ☐ 7 ☐ 8 ☐ 9 ☐ 10

NOTES:

OVERNIGHT CHARGE – JOURNAL ENTRY #5			
DATE	BED TIME	WAKE TIME	TOTAL TIME
DID YOU WAKE UP EARLIER THAN YOU INTENDED?		☐ YES	☐ NO
HOW RESTED ARE YOU ON A SCALE OF 1 to 10?			
☐ 1 ☐ 2 ☐ 3 ☐ 4 ☐ 5 ☐ 6 ☐ 7 ☐ 8 ☐ 9 ☐ 10			
NOTES			

OVERNIGHT CHARGE – JOURNAL ENTRY #6			
DATE	BED TIME	WAKE TIME	TOTAL TIME
DID YOU WAKE UP EARLIER THAN YOU INTENDED?		☐ YES	☐ NO
HOW RESTED ARE YOU ON A SCALE OF 1 to 10?			
☐ 1 ☐ 2 ☐ 3 ☐ 4 ☐ 5 ☐ 6 ☐ 7 ☐ 8 ☐ 9 ☐ 10			
NOTES			

OVERNIGHT CHARGE – JOURNAL ENTRY #7			
DATE	BED TIME	WAKE TIME	TOTAL TIME
DID YOU WAKE UP EARLIER THAN YOU INTENDED?		☐ YES	☐ NO
HOW RESTED ARE YOU ON A SCALE OF 1 to 10?			
☐ 1 ☐ 2 ☐ 3 ☐ 4 ☐ 5 ☐ 6 ☐ 7 ☐ 8 ☐ 9 ☐ 10			
NOTES			

OVERNIGHT CHARGE – JOURNAL ENTRY #8			
DATE	BED TIME	WAKE TIME	TOTAL TIME
DID YOU WAKE UP EARLIER THAN YOU INTENDED?		☐ YES	☐ NO
HOW RESTED ARE YOU ON A SCALE OF 1 to 10?			
☐ 1 ☐ 2 ☐ 3 ☐ 4 ☐ 5 ☐ 6 ☐ 7 ☐ 8 ☐ 9 ☐ 10			
NOTES			

OVERNIGHT CHARGE – JOURNAL ENTRY #9

DATE	BED TIME	WAKE TIME	TOTAL TIME

DID YOU WAKE UP EARLIER THAN YOU INTENDED? ☐ YES ☐ NO

HOW RESTED ARE YOU ON A SCALE OF 1 to 10?

☐	☐	☐	☐	☐	☐	☐	☐	☐	☐
1	2	3	4	5	6	7	8	9	10

NOTES

OVERNIGHT CHARGE – JOURNAL ENTRY #10

DATE	BED TIME	WAKE TIME	TOTAL TIME

DID YOU WAKE UP EARLIER THAN YOU INTENDED? ☐ YES ☐ NO

HOW RESTED ARE YOU ON A SCALE OF 1 to 10?

☐	☐	☐	☐	☐	☐	☐	☐	☐	☐
1	2	3	4	5	6	7	8	9	10

NOTES

OVERNIGHT CHARGE – JOURNAL ENTRY #11

DATE	BED TIME	WAKE TIME	TOTAL TIME

DID YOU WAKE UP EARLIER THAN YOU INTENDED? ☐ YES ☐ NO

HOW RESTED ARE YOU ON A SCALE OF 1 to 10?

☐	☐	☐	☐	☐	☐	☐	☐	☐	☐
1	2	3	4	5	6	7	8	9	10

NOTES

OVERNIGHT CHARGE – JOURNAL ENTRY #12

DATE	BED TIME	WAKE TIME	TOTAL TIME

DID YOU WAKE UP EARLIER THAN YOU INTENDED? ☐ YES ☐ NO

HOW RESTED ARE YOU ON A SCALE OF 1 to 10?

☐	☐	☐	☐	☐	☐	☐	☐	☐	☐
1	2	3	4	5	6	7	8	9	10

NOTES

OVERNIGHT CHARGE – JOURNAL ENTRY #13

DATE	BED TIME	WAKE TIME	TOTAL TIME

DID YOU WAKE UP EARLIER THAN YOU INTENDED? ☐ YES ☐ NO

HOW RESTED ARE YOU ON A SCALE OF 1 to 10?

☐ 1 ☐ 2 ☐ 3 ☐ 4 ☐ 5 ☐ 6 ☐ 7 ☐ 8 ☐ 9 ☐ 10

NOTES:

OVERNIGHT CHARGE – JOURNAL ENTRY #14

DATE	BED TIME	WAKE TIME	TOTAL TIME

DID YOU WAKE UP EARLIER THAN YOU INTENDED? ☐ YES ☐ NO

HOW RESTED ARE YOU ON A SCALE OF 1 to 10?

☐ 1 ☐ 2 ☐ 3 ☐ 4 ☐ 5 ☐ 6 ☐ 7 ☐ 8 ☐ 9 ☐ 10

NOTES:

OVERNIGHT CHARGE – JOURNAL ENTRY #15

DATE	BED TIME	WAKE TIME	TOTAL TIME

DID YOU WAKE UP EARLIER THAN YOU INTENDED? ☐ YES ☐ NO

HOW RESTED ARE YOU ON A SCALE OF 1 to 10?

☐ 1 ☐ 2 ☐ 3 ☐ 4 ☐ 5 ☐ 6 ☐ 7 ☐ 8 ☐ 9 ☐ 10

NOTES:

OVERNIGHT CHARGE – JOURNAL ENTRY #16

DATE	BED TIME	WAKE TIME	TOTAL TIME

DID YOU WAKE UP EARLIER THAN YOU INTENDED? ☐ YES ☐ NO

HOW RESTED ARE YOU ON A SCALE OF 1 to 10?

☐ 1 ☐ 2 ☐ 3 ☐ 4 ☐ 5 ☐ 6 ☐ 7 ☐ 8 ☐ 9 ☐ 10

NOTES:

OVERNIGHT CHARGE – JOURNAL ENTRY #17

DATE	BED TIME	WAKE TIME	TOTAL TIME

DID YOU WAKE UP EARLIER THAN YOU INTENDED? ☐ YES ☐ NO

HOW RESTED ARE YOU ON A SCALE OF 1 to 10?

☐ 1 ☐ 2 ☐ 3 ☐ 4 ☐ 5 ☐ 6 ☐ 7 ☐ 8 ☐ 9 ☐ 10

NOTES

OVERNIGHT CHARGE – JOURNAL ENTRY #18

DATE	BED TIME	WAKE TIME	TOTAL TIME

DID YOU WAKE UP EARLIER THAN YOU INTENDED? ☐ YES ☐ NO

HOW RESTED ARE YOU ON A SCALE OF 1 to 10?

☐ 1 ☐ 2 ☐ 3 ☐ 4 ☐ 5 ☐ 6 ☐ 7 ☐ 8 ☐ 9 ☐ 10

NOTES

OVERNIGHT CHARGE – JOURNAL ENTRY #19

DATE	BED TIME	WAKE TIME	TOTAL TIME

DID YOU WAKE UP EARLIER THAN YOU INTENDED? ☐ YES ☐ NO

HOW RESTED ARE YOU ON A SCALE OF 1 to 10?

☐ 1 ☐ 2 ☐ 3 ☐ 4 ☐ 5 ☐ 6 ☐ 7 ☐ 8 ☐ 9 ☐ 10

NOTES

OVERNIGHT CHARGE – JOURNAL ENTRY #20

DATE	BED TIME	WAKE TIME	TOTAL TIME

DID YOU WAKE UP EARLIER THAN YOU INTENDED? ☐ YES ☐ NO

HOW RESTED ARE YOU ON A SCALE OF 1 to 10?

☐ 1 ☐ 2 ☐ 3 ☐ 4 ☐ 5 ☐ 6 ☐ 7 ☐ 8 ☐ 9 ☐ 10

NOTES

NOTES

Chapter Eleven

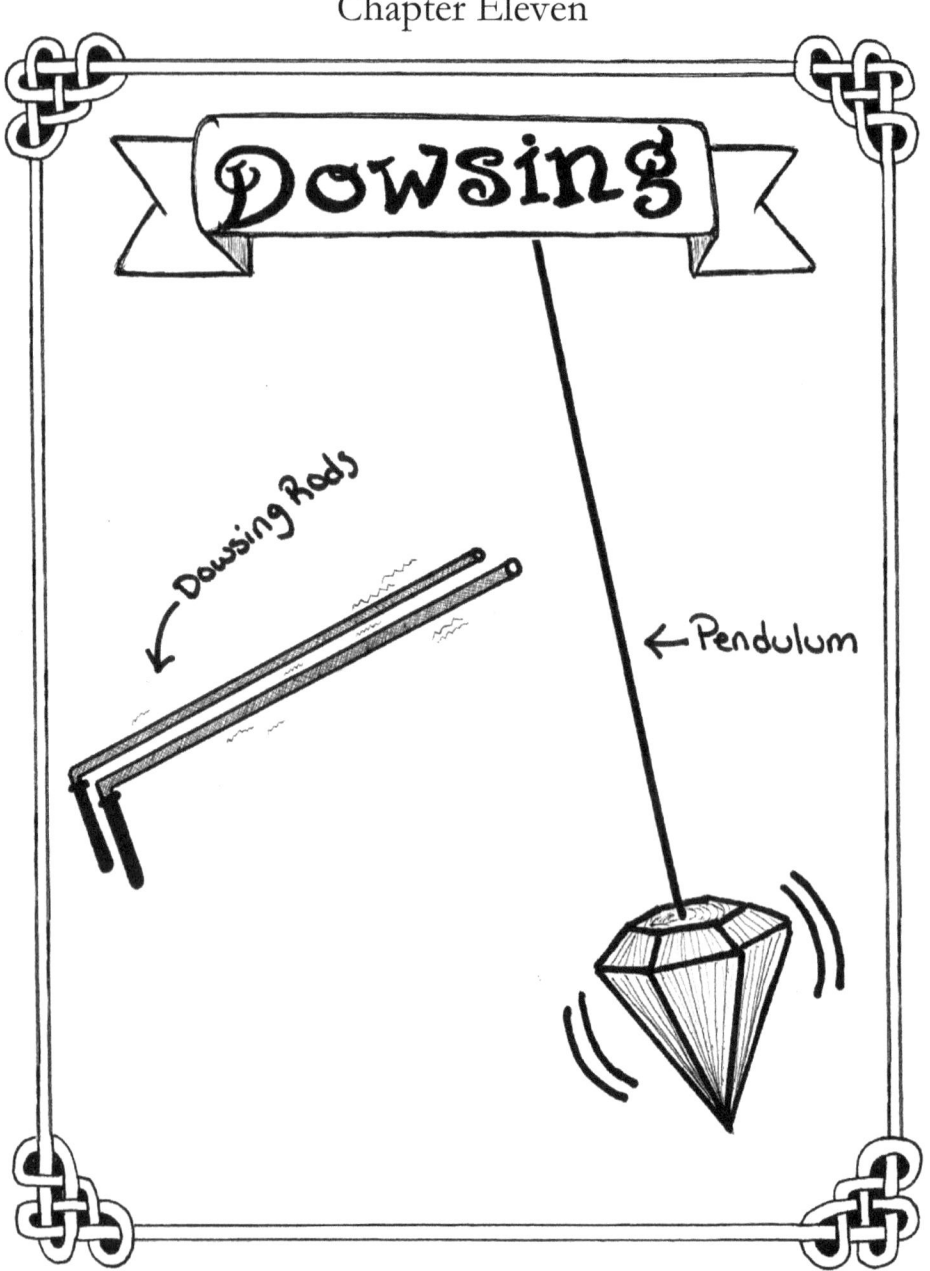

Dowsing

← Dowsing Rods

← Pendulum

A divination tool that can answer your questions, help find lost items and speak with spirits.

DOWSING

Skill level : Medium
Estimated Time: 10-15 min

Possible Tools

- Dowsing Rods: *Can be purchased or made by bending a metal clothing hanger into an L-shape as depicted on the left.*

- Pendulum: *Can be purchased or made by suspending a weight, crystal or stone from a string or chain. See drawing on the left.*

Directions

1. **Cleanse** your rods or pendulum. To do this, sit on the floor or ground. Hold the device to your heart with one hand and place your other hand on the floor. Close your eyes and visualize all energy draining from the device, through your body and into the ground. When you feel your dowsing device is clear of any energy, continue holding it to your heart (now with both hands) and allow it to align itself with your vibration. Alternate methods involve burying your device in the ground overnight, smudging it with sage, sprinkling it with holy water or soaking it in saltwater.

2. **Determine** your source and purpose. Will you be working with your own energy or a spirit's energy? Are you looking for the answer to a specific question or do you need help locating something? Be sure to vocalize this intention out loud. If you're going to work with energies other than your own, establish that you are only interested in making contact with that which has your best interest at heart. Additionally, you may wish to declare that contact only be made through the dowsing device. Some people are okay with energies touching them or moving things, though it's recommended you establish physical boundaries.

3. **Calibrate** your rods or pendulum. To do this, ask the device to show you what a "yes" and a "no" look like. If you're using rods, they will likely make an "X" or point outwards. If you're using a pendulum, it may rotate clockwise, counter-clockwise, swing left to right or front to back. After you've determined what "yes" and "no" look like, ask a simple question you already know the answer to. *Example: Is my name Steven?* Be sure that you are shown the correct answer. It's recommended that you do this before each use – especially if you're working with different energies that may show their answers differently. Next, ask to be shown what the "neutral" position looks like. This way, after asking questions, you can ask your device to return to neutral. Lastly (if you're using rods), you can ask to be pointed in the direction of a particular room or item.

4. **Dowse**. You're now ready to begin dowsing. Focus your energy and intentions on the device and allow the rods or pendulum to do the rest! If you're searching for something lost you may want to incorporate additional tools like a map.

Dowsing Uses

Historically, dowsing has most commonly been used to find natural resources like water, minerals, gold and oil. Some professionals enjoy incorporating dowsing as an aid with missing persons cases, holistic healing and psychology. On a daily basis, you may find dowsing a helpful tool when searching for lost items, seeking guidance on a particular situation, balancing Chakras or speaking with spirit guides.

Note from the author

Personally, I enjoy dowsing, as it provides a visual to accompany and validate the information I receive intuitively. If you're speaking with other energies, remind yourself that you never know whom you're dealing with - you could easily be misled or receive responses from your subconscious frequencies. However you do it, have fun and make a point to journal your experiences along the way!

NOTES

Chapter Twelve

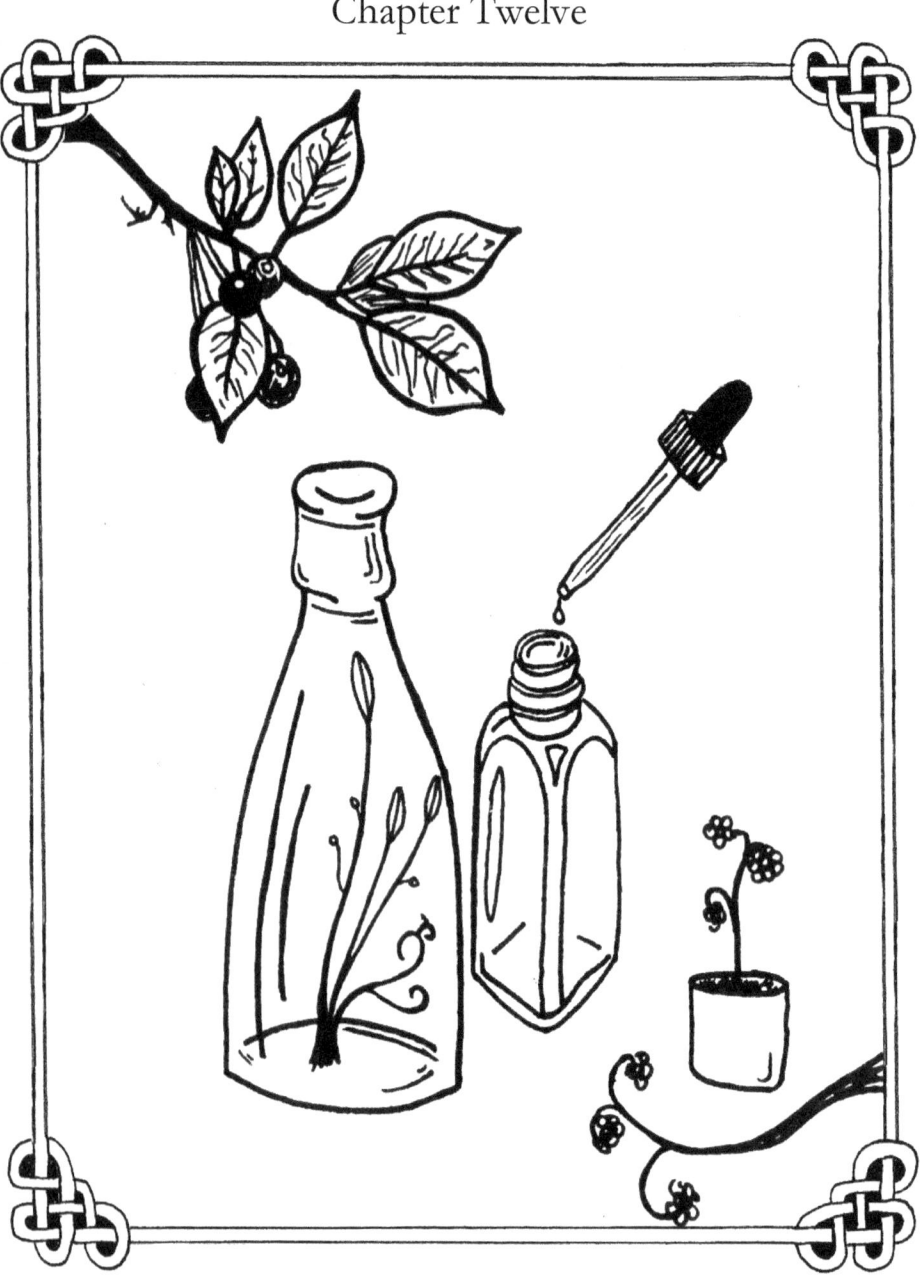

The elemental gifts from our earth have powerful healing, psychic and protective properties.

ESSENTIAL OILS

From sacred rituals to aromatherapy massage, Essential Oils have long been used to help mankind. Before science and religion, oils were extracted from trees, plants, flowers and fruit to treat illness, offered as gifts and believed to hold magic powers. In modern day, science developments have helped to understand the physiological responses to various oils. Metaphysically, Essential Oils are used for everything from promoting psychic awareness to balancing chakra energy.

The most common techniques for integrating Essential Oils into your life include: heating a few drops using an oil burner, mixing some into a soothing bath, topical application during a massage, placing a few drops on a cloth under your pillow when sleeping (for the smell), hanging some on scent diffuser for the car or simply putting some on as a substitute to perfume or cologne. In some cases, people prefer to ingest essential oils so their body can directly reap the benefits – this is not recommended, nor will this method be discussed in this chapter. It's important to note that while essential oils are generally safe for use, some are considered toxic when ingested. Even small doses of natural oils are highly concentrated and can be dangerous when entering the blood stream. Additionally, be sure that you're only using pure essential oils as synthetic essential oils do not have the same healing properties.

While the individual benefits of certain oils are commonly accepted, your experience may vary. As you experiment with different oils, you may find that certain scents are more irritating while others are more soothing simply based on preference. This should not discredit the healing properties of essential oils – like medication, people respond differently despite the intended outcome. In this chapter, you will find a list of oils and their common uses. You are also being provided a log to journal your experience with the essential oils that you try!

<u>Disclaimer</u>

The information provided in this chapter is not dispelled as medical advice. Please consult a professional if you require assistance.

ESSENTIAL OIL	METAPHYSICAL USES
Basil	Assists when you're clashing personalities with someone else. Can be worn when in large crowds for protection. Is very freeing from infidelity, spells and bad luck.
Bayberry	Manifests luck & money.
Bergamot	Provides protection from harm.
Black Pepper	Gets rid of people with wicked intentions. Raises courage and enhances the potential of other essential oils when mixed together.
Cedarwood	Brings confidence and protects from all that brings misery (including misfortune).
Cinnamon	Great for enhancing psychic abilities. Raises and enhances your vibration while promoting concentration which helps stimulate clairvoyance.
Citronella	Aside from scaring away bugs, it actually attracts both friends and customers.
Clove	Helps to strengthen your memory and is protective from both negative forces and thoughts.
Cypress	Useful in times of transition. Promotes a long and healthy life. Also helps to translate sexual energy into a more spiritual energy.
Eucalyptus	Deals with healing emotions and depression. Is also soothing in times of illness.
Fennel	Protects your energy field (aura) and establishes boundaries. Strengthens your influence over other people. Protects from negative spells.
Frankincense	Helps to release destructive habits. Exorcises negative energy (purifying) and helps to protect from those energies in the future. Brings luck.
Geranium	Possess the closest yin/yang balance of all the oils. Can be used to integrate duality into your energy. Strengthens the connections with spiritual people.
Ginger	Helps to stimulate kundalini energy and other forms of self-awareness.
Grapefruit	Rids feelings of self-doubt by raising confidence. Helps to deal with jealousy, envy and frustration.
Honeysuckle	Releases past regrets so that you can move forward in your life. Attracts various forms of abundance.

Jasmine	Cleanses the aura and provides psychic protection. Helps to stimulate creativity and originality. Is also believed to attract spiritual love.
Juniper	Has the ability to transform emotions and a clearer way of thinking. Purifies the physical and energetic bodies. Attracts justice and guards from enemies.
Lavender	Assists with achieving inner peace in all ways. Frees from emotional stress and gives increased awareness. Brings more permanent stability.
Lemongrass	Conjures protective spirits.
Myrrh	Helps with understanding personal grief to bring peace – also guards against evil that prevents that.
Orange	Brings harmony and balance to raise inner power.
Peppermint	Is great for purifying the atmosphere in buildings (both personal and professional establishments). Raises the overall vibration of a place. Useful after trauma to overcome dark emotions. Add to other oils to increase their potency.
Pine	Cleanses to end false allegations.
Rose	Attracts unconditional love and peace. Creates a more harmonic and tranquil dynamic in relationships and within.
Rosemary	Protective.
Sage	An alternative from the smokiness of burning a sage stick. Powerful in clearing and cleansing. Sage removes all negative energies.
Sandalwood	Great for stimulating clairvoyance and for looking into past lives. Is very healing and known to clear, calm and protect the mind.
Sweetgrass	Aids in personal transformation and attracts spiritual blessings on the way.
Vetiver	Helps you release your emotions and fears so that you can fully embrace what it is that you want in life. If you've had continuous bad luck, this can break that pattern. Is also used in many love and prosperity spells.

Date

Oil / Combination

Notes

Date

Oil / Combination

Notes

Date

Oil / Combination

Notes

THE DIVINITY DOCTRINE

Date
Oil / Combination
Notes

Date
Oil / Combination
Notes

Date
Oil / Combination
Notes

Chapter Thirteen

Grounding is a great way to keep yourself level-headed and energetically balanced.

GROUNDING

Whether you're feeling scattered or need to balance your energy, grounding is one of the easiest and most helpful practices included in this book. When life gets chaotic or when your thoughts are "up in the clouds", taking a few minutes to bring yourself back into perspective can make the world of a difference. While "taking a deep breath" may be something you already do, there are many other effective ways to re-connect with your most authentic state of being.

Metaphysically, grounding techniques are essential when working with energy. For those who are sensitive or empathic, grounding can be helpful when looking to flush out the thoughts, emotions and energies you've accumulated from others so that you can regain perspective. For psychics and mediums, grounding can be practiced before sessions to offer clarity and after sessions to bring yourself back to a more human state of being. Grounding can also bridge the gap between dimensions.

In earlier chapters, the use of crystals to achieve inner balance has already been discussed. While crystals can be a great tool for grounding, this chapter is designed to outline techniques based on visualization and lifestyle adjustments.

Symptoms

There are a variety of ways which your mind and body might be telling you that it needs grounding. While many of the symptoms can be linked to physical or psychological illness, grounding yourself can be a great addition to your daily regiment to help keep yourself levelheaded and energetically balanced. The most common symptoms that reflect you're not grounded enough include: *Random emotions/thoughts that don't reflect your current situation, feeling unfocused or zoned out, struggling to communicate your thoughts clearly, your eyes are twitching or your feel uncomfortable vibrations throughout your body, clumsiness, being more forgetful than usual, cold hands, heart palpitations, falling asleep when meditating or feeling tired after a good night sleep.*

Tree Grounding

Many times, trees have inhabited earth longer than we have. As the seasons change and as time passes us by, they stand quietly – listening and observing. With their roots running deep into the ground, they're directly connected to this dimensions most powerful energy source (earth). The same way that trees absorb our carbon dioxide and convert it into oxygen to give us life, trees are also capable of absorbing negativity to help restore your mind, body and energy.

For this exercise, stand outside underneath a solid tree. Extending your arms outward, place your hands on the base of the tree and close your eyes. Breathing deeply, visualize the tree like an advanced system of veins that connect from your body, through your hands, through the tree and into the earth. Below your feet, feel the ground and see the same veins connecting you to the earth – almost like your own set of roots. There is a gold light that moves quickly through the veins. This gold light is natural energy and unbiased wisdom. You are now tapping into truth and displacing your thoughts from ego. The longer your hands are on the tree, the faster this gold light fills your body. With every breath in, the gold light pulsates brighter. With every breath out, your body releases any stress in a thick black smog. As you release any energetic pollution from your body, see the smog getting thinner and clearer. Continue this exercise until you visualize a clear breath out and feel fully charged with the earths energy.

This exercise is especially helpful in restoring your mind, body, and spirit to its most natural state of being. As we come into contact with negative people and experiences, our perception is altered which can impair our ability to function properly/normally. This technique is designed to clear any emotional and spiritual pollution from the body while replacing it with the earths pure energy.

Something you may consider adding to this technique is imagining a metallic cord connecting your head to the sky above. With this, you are now connected to both the purity of the earth and the knowledge from "source". This can be especially helpful before performing a psychic reading or when looking for clarity and guidance on a situation. Overall, this helps to balance the energy flow between the crown chakra (which connects with the divine) and root chakra (which provides grounding).

Chakra Elevator Technique

With most chakra meditations, people focus their energy starting at the root chakra and work upward to the crown chakra, which helps with raising your vibration. When looking to ground yourself and to stabilize your vibration (bringing you back to earth), you start with the crown chakra and work downward to the root chakra.

Begin by sitting comfortably on the floor and close your eyes. Visualize your chakra system as if it was floors on an elevator. Starting at the crown chakra, you press all of the buttons in the elevator. Before the doors close, you look down and notice how high up are you from the ground. You're able to see the "bigger picture" of things, but look forward to joining everyone else on the streets. Before the doors close, exhale deeply to allow all built up energy to escape. Allowing all anxiety and built up energy to escape at each chakra that you stop on, you feel more and more comfortable. As you get closer to the ground level (root chakra) allow yourself to feel more and more in touch with the world you were earlier looking down at. Once you have reached the root chakra, open your eyes as the doors open. You're now free to travel the same streets as everyone else. You no longer see things from "above" and can instead see what is right ahead of you.

This technique is especially helpful when you feel like your chakras have been oversensitive or when you're overwhelmed with possibilities. Like looking towards the horizon from the top floor of a building, it can be overpowering when you see the complex network of streets/possibility. Allowing yourself to see things from the ground level, you're still able to see things as they come but can deal with things more head on. The purpose of "stopping at each floor" is to allow any built up energy to escape your chakras. By doing this, you release the anxieties that can manifest from particular chakra overloads.

For information on chakra overload and deficiency symptoms, you may consider reading the "chakra" chapter.

Dietary Grounding

On a day-to-day basis, it can be difficult to find time for visualization techniques. Allowing nutritional and spiritual needs to go unmet for extended amounts of time, the body will eventually find ways to produce a psychological response that translates into hunger. Many times, when people need grounding, they find themselves craving red meat, chocolate and wine. Aside from the vibrational patterns these products carry, meat (for example) carries animal (instinctual and maternal) energy which can be very grounding. This is why people often rely on food for comfort. Without being gluttonous, identifying and satisfying the cravings from your body can aid with day to day grounding. When your heart chakra is out of balance, this doesn't mean to eat a ton of chocolate – vegetables that correlate to that chakra's color (green) are most helpful. Scientifically speaking, colors are the frequency translation of a colors vibration. By ingesting foods that match certain chakra colors, you're recharging those chakras in one of the most direct ways possible.

Activity Changes

Ever wonder why some people find doing the dishes or vacuuming therapeutic? When we get more hands on with things, we're able to ground ourselves by focusing on the things that require our attention on a more human level. If you find cleaning to be stressful, some alternates you might consider include: walking to connect with nature (either by yourself or with a dog), gardening, sports, yoga, swimming, art, etc. Listen to your body and see how it feels. If you're lacking sleep and your thoughts are racing, going for a jog might not be the best idea - sometimes taking a quick nap might be just what you need. Lastly, getting a massage can also be very helpful in stepping away from your thoughts, relaxing and identifying yourself in a more physical sense.

NOTES

Chapter Fourteen

Law of Attraction

You can have almost anything you want in life.
The trick is learning how to attract it!

LAW OF ATTRACTION

If someone told you that everything in your life was a direct result of your thoughts and emotions, what would you say? How would you feel in knowing that you were singlehandedly responsible for attracting everything good and bad into your life? One could look at their life and feel empowered to know their fate is in their own hands. Another could look at their current situation and feel victimized. How could their thoughts have had any influence on the parking ticket the received or the traffic they hit on the way to work? And even if it was that easy to manifest your thoughts, why haven't you won the lottery yet, right? If it was that easy, wouldn't everyone be happy, healthy and wealthy?

Scientifically speaking, it's commonly accepted that every action you make causes some type of reaction. With that, the positive or negative nature of your actions will greatly influence the type of reaction you receive in return. Put out kindness and you're more likely to receive a smile or "thank you" from someone. Put out bitterness and disrespect and you're likely to be gossiped about, avoided, or treated poorly in return. But how do your thoughts play into things? Take the simple action of standing up for example. Before you can physically stand, it was a thought first. Your brain first requires thoughts to translate them into bodily actions (a reaction to your thoughts). Even thinking about standing, but not doing so, is a result of your thoughts. Inaction is action because you're choosing "not to act" which is an action within itself.

The next step is understanding how your unspoken thoughts affect everything and everyone around you. With every thought, your brain produces a measurable brainwave frequency. Whether you're reading, sleeping, speaking or eating, you're emitting brainwaves. Thousands of neurons carrying electricity scatter around with every conscious and unconscious thought. Positive thoughts and excitement carry a higher energetic frequency and negative thoughts and sadness carry a lower energetic frequency. This isn't a metaphysical interpretation/opinion - it has been proven by science. Recognizing the energetic power of your brain, you can begin to imagine how your thoughts affect others. Every time you think something, you're exerting positive or negative energy.

Quantum Physics (science that deals with energy) supports the concept that "like attracts like". This law is called the "Law of Attraction". Understanding the energy your thoughts carry, you can now apply the Law of Attraction and see how much influence you have over what you attract to your life. Positive thoughts output high vibrations that will attract people and situations that carry the same higher frequency. On the contrary, negative thoughts output lower vibrations that will attract people and situations that carry the same lower (negative) frequency. By simply adjusting your thoughts (and actions), your life can slowly begin transforming into what you always imagined it could be.

If you consider yourself a generally positive person, you might be wondering why you're experiencing some negative situations. Life contracts aside, you have to take into consideration the way you think positive thoughts. Let's pretend for example you're living month to month (you're very tight on money). You tell yourself that "it's okay, someday things will be better". Generally, one would assume that's a positive attitude, right? Wrong. While it's positive that you're not allowing your situation to get the worst of you, that does not imply your thoughts are carrying a high frequency. When you output energy that something will be better in the future, the universe will return it to you that same way – something in the future. Remember, like attracts like. By visualizing stability in the future, your brain is outputting that energy to the world around you.

By shifting your way of thinking, your brain can begin emitting higher frequency brainwaves that will attract people and situations that carry that same (positive) frequency. To do this, begin visualizing the things you desire as though you already have them. Visualization is thought and thoughts carry brainwaves. If you desire stability, regularly imagine already having it. As you visualize the flexibility and freedom that comes with being financially stable, imagine experiencing the emotions that come with having those things. Emotions carry a very strong electromagnetic response that is slightly higher than thoughts alone. The more you can visualize having emotional responses to things (as though you already have them), the stronger you will emit your intentions so that they can begin manifesting in your life. If you can do this while also making positive choices (actions) in your life, you should begin seeing rapid changes in your life.

Aside from thinking about things in the future, the second mistake that people make (to attract negative things) is focusing energy on what it is that they don't want. Pretend you're in a rush for work. If you begin thinking "I hope I don't hit traffic on the way", it's likely you will actually attract traffic. The universe doesn't decipher what you do or don't want. You send out brainwaves associated with the visualization of hitting traffic – the universe simply returns it. This is why many times, when you're in a rush, you hit every stop light. While it can be intimidating thinking about how quickly a simple thought can manifest, it's nothing to be scared about. Allow it to be empowering in knowing that you hold the power over what it is you attract into your life.

To speed up the process of manifestation, you can use other earthly and scientific laws to your advantage. Using gravity as an example, if you release a pendulum from one side, it will swing and then return. With the things that you desire, release any pressures from achieving them so that they can return when they're ready. Along the way, be conscious of what you've asked for and how it fits into your life. Many times, the "losses" you experience are eliminated to make way for the things you're attempting to manifest. The mistake people make is getting caught in the emotion from "losing something", which then shifts their vibration to attracting more loss before they can reap the benefits from the change that was happening. If you ask for the opportunity to live a prosperous life, for example, you may experience a job termination or breakup to make way for a higher paying job or spouse that better aligns with what you desire. The people, places and situations that do not carry the same frequency will drop away as quantum physics takes place and like attracts like. The same can be said if you're thinking negatively; you will lose the things that are positive and be surrounded with negative people and hard situations.

All in all, the best advice that I can give to you is to simply take things as they are. Release the need to define things as positive or negative and simply accept them as just being. I'm not saying that you have to just accept crummy things in your life – it means you accept they're part of your life now for a reason (without getting down about it) and shift your thoughts to a more positive state of being to attract better things in the future. Along the way, release the need to determine how things "should" be. Many times, there are better paths than we've even imagined. What you're enduring may simply be one of those occasions.

Techniques for Manifesting

There is literally an infinite number of ways to manifest the things you desire through the law of attraction. The following are some techniques to consider giving a try:

Create a Vision board

Begin by cutting out pictures of all the things you love and desire. Next, paste your clippings onto a poster board or piece of paper. You can make your board as simple or fancy as you'd like. Hang this somewhere you will see it every day. If a poster board isn't convenient size wise and you use a notebook daily, you can also make a collage on the cover! Every time that you see your vision board or collage, look at the pictures and lose yourself in them. Invest your energy in visualizing what it's like already having the things pictured.

Gratitude Jar/Box

Find a clear jar or a small shoe box (if you'd like to decorate the outside). Every time that something positive or fun happens, write it on a small piece of paper, fold it and place it inside your jar/box. Aside from the notes you write, you might find it fun to include fortune cookie notes, movie tickets, news clippings, etc. One year later (or on New Year's Eve), open your jar/box and read all of its contents. The goal in mind to remind yourself of the positive things that happened and offer gratitude. This will attract more positivity into your life!

Meditation

Each day as you wake up (or fall asleep), meditate and visualize the things you desire as though you already have them. If things are taking longer than you expected to manifest, research a guided meditation for manifestation that encourages the release and return of what you desire. Release the pressures you've accumulated from your mind so it can output higher frequency thoughts to attract higher frequency people, places and situations.

NOTES

Chapter Fifteen

Discover your purpose and where you come from.
There's more to life than you think.

LIFE CONTRACTS

Have you ever questioned the point of life? Sometimes things move so slow it's unbearable and other times life passes you by. Along the way, people commonly spend their life pondering what their destiny is. What were they made for? What will they accomplish? Even in the end, it's easy to ask what role your existence played in the scheme of things. In your hands, you hold a powerful tool – the answer to many of these questions. While I do not claim to possess all of life's answers, the information I'm providing has been accumulated through my years of experience as a psychic-medium. Keeping in mind that we're all on different journeys, this chapter should serve as a stepping stone in simply working towards recognizing your individual purpose.

Before coming into the third dimension, we were created through an energetic transformation on "the other side". While there isn't enough vocabulary on earth to adequately express my understanding of what we were, my perception of our physical composition translates easiest to little balls of white light. While we had a consciousness, we weren't designed with a full understanding of life – instead, created with the intention of fulfilling it.

Engraved with the emotional capacity to embrace free-will, we were presented with a variety of life contracts which we'd have to choose from. Like reading the synopsis on the back of a book, we were able to read an outline of different lives without knowing all of its details. While some of the contracts discussed easy walks of life, they were lengthy and required more time on earth to learn the lessons necessary. Others were full of challenges, but required less of our time on earth as we'd learn more about our purpose in a shorter amount of time.

Detailing the personal qualities we'd adapt and the situations we'd have to encounter, we now had what we needed to begin our journey on earth. Matched to families with compatible contracts, we were carefully placed in order to fulfill each-others commitments. From there on out, we would have as much time (and as many lifetimes) as needed to achieve an understanding of life and our purpose.

While the interpretation I've shared with you so far may not align with your religious understanding, simply reading this chapter may have even been a contracted experience to challenge your way of thinking. Even though many of our experiences are pre-determined, it is also important to note that we have free-will in choosing how we fulfill our contract. Perhaps stumbling upon this book was a result of "chance" from a decision founded on free-will. Whichever option it is that's allowed me to cross paths with you, we are now part of each-others journeys. It's amazing how fast things change!

Reading about contracted experiences and those of free-will, you may be wondering how to identify the two. The truth is, many of the times that we feel as though we're acting out of free-will, our decision was already made before this lifetime. That aside, if you're experiencing something difficult in your life, there is a clear way of knowing whether it was contracted or a path you chose in this lifetime. If you have a feeling that something you're going to do will end up bad (but you decide to do it anyway), it was likely a contracted experience. Your intuition comes from a "sense of knowing" as you've already seen how the situation will play out when you were in the spirit world. Your physical body isn't aware of this however, so it does what it was programmed to do (despite knowing it wouldn't end well). This is why I always tell people to release the need to determine things as good or bad – they just are. Each experience is designed to get you where you need to be. The same way that you couldn't predict all of the hardships that have come your way, you can't see all of the good ahead either.

Keeping in mind that time was created by man, the duration of your contracted experience isn't something that can be measured. You have all of the "time" you need to achieve the understanding necessary to ascend to the next dimension. Many times, the reason we see children die young (or miscarriages) from freak situations is because one of the parents was contracted to experience loss and the child was an old soul coming back to wrap up their contract. While this is not always the case, sometimes things just happen and there's no explanation. I use this scenario however to reiterate the fact that time in this dimension means nothing when it comes to fulfilling our purpose. We cannot ascend until we have a rounded perspective and can fully appreciate the dimension we'd be embracing. For more information detailing the ascension process, please visit chapter three.

Your Contract

So, how does all of this information help you now? We're going to discuss two ways that you can actually tap into your life contract to better understand how to fulfill your life purpose.

Past Life Regression

Used as a tool to help revisit your other lifetimes, Past Life Regression (PLR) is especially helpful when looking for insight into behavioral patterns and personality traits. Often, if you were previously not able to complete your contract, certain qualities might resurface in your current life. When you can identify reoccurring patters, it can be especially beneficial in understanding why your contract went unfulfilled in the past. It can also be helpful in deciding what you'd like to do differently in this lifetime or why you feel a certain way about a current situation. While PLR can be achieved independently, I encourage you to seek a specialist if this is something you're interested in pursuing.

Akashic Records

Every past event, contracted future event and independent life blueprint/contract is held in a protected "library" in the next dimension. Through mediation, astral projection or consulting your guides, those who are spiritually developed may be granted access to the Akashic Records. Though certain isles are off limits to "civilians", many of the issues you'd be seeking insight on are readily accessible. While most people enjoy reading through the scrolls and books, not everyone has an easy time achieving astral projection in the first place. For this, the most common way to attain the knowledge found within the Akashic Records is to meditate or ask your guides. When doing this, you may be gifted a sense of "knowing" or even be gifted the records while sleeping (in the dream state). Remember that what you want to know versus what you need to know may also dictate which information you're shown. Sometimes you just have to have a little faith and trust God.

Chapter Sixteen

Talking boards can be a very useful tool.
The trick is knowing how to use them.

OUIJA BOARDS

Also referred to as a talking board or a spirit board, Ouija Boards were initially introduced as a parlor game. It wasn't until the 1900's that they became mainstreamed as divination tools. While some religions consider the Ouija demonic, modern game companies have developed new versions that can be found in almost any toy store.

Used to seek answers, Ouija Boards are believed to provide a platform for spirits to communicate with the human world. Culturally, there are many variations for talking boards, though the one pictured on the left has become most popular. Generally made out of wood or cardboard, most spirit boards possess the letters of the alphabet, numbers, yes and no. When used, participants place their fingers on a piece known as a planchette which then slides over the board to spell out words for answer the questions being asked.

Scientifically there has been a large debate surrounding the authenticity of whether or not Ouija Boards are real. Many psychologists believe that the participants are actually subconsciously moving the piece, while others have acknowledged a faulty participant could easily manipulate the planchette.

Though my own personal experience and with the help of my guides, I have reached the conclusion that Ouija Boards themselves carry no special power. As with any time you create an opportunity for spirit to communicate, the tools in which you use simply become a medium for communication. For this, it is my belief that many of the ideas surrounding how to effectively use a Ouija Board are man-made myths.

Initially, I was conflicted on whether or not to include this chapter as I've had my fair share of negative experiences with Ouija Boards. In the end, I concluded the purpose of this chapter would be to provide cautionary information and suggestions to make your experience a little smoother (should you choose to try one). While I will not endorse or discourage the use of Talking Boards, I believe that it is my job to simply provide the information so you can reach your own conclusion.

Safety Precautions

1. If you plan to use a Ouija Board and are feeling negative or afraid, it is my recommendation that you don't use one. Should you come into contact with a spirit, you do not want to be susceptible to any energetic influence. Additionally, when you're operating from fear, you carry a low vibration which attracts spirits with low-vibrations (negative spirits).

2. Always establish your intentions and limitations. Personally, I always vocalize that beyond the board, I do not give any spirit permission to make physical contact or move things. When I end the session, I ask that contact is to be ceased (though as a medium, I have a difficult time establishing this boundary as a board is not necessary to communicate).

3. If at any time the board begins swearing, getting angry, disrespectful or tried to disturb you, close your session and discontinue use. This is not to say that you should be afraid, but you should make a conscious effort to protect yourself from allowing any negative entity influence over your thoughts, emotions or behaviors.

4. Remember that you are never really sure who you're speaking with. Even though you may ask a spirit to identify itself, they can say anything they like. For that, do not accept anything the board says as complete truth. If you're looking for insight into a situation, be aware you could easily be misled/lied to. Ouija Boards are not an Oracle and should not be treated as one.

5. Know your audience. If you are seriously intending to connect with a spirit, simply be aware of who the other participants are. Despite someone promising not to push the planchette, it is always a possibility that someone is directing the responses. This is yet another reason that I take what the board says with a grain of salt.

6. Though your home may be the only place you're able to use a talking board, it is my suggestion you avoid doing so. Your home is intended to be your sanctuary – if you have a negative experience, you need a place to return where you can feel safe.

7. Always close your session, even if you have to manually move the planchette to "goodbye". I also like to ground and protect myself after.

Make Your Own

- Find a piece of paper or cardboard and replicate the letter and number placement seen on the image at the beginning of this chapter.

- In substitute of a planchette, you can use an upside-down shot glass which should slide easily around the paper.

- If you try sliding the shot glass around and the paper bunches up, tape the edges of the paper to the table or floor to secure it.

Chapter Seventeen

What does it mean to be Psychic?
Uncover your hidden potential.

PSYCHICS

Message from the Author

As a Psychic-Medium myself, this is one of the chapters I was most excited about including! While this handbook is intended to serve as a reference guide, I've done my best to exclude my personal opinions in order to provide a more authentic learning experience. As you read about the different types of spiritual gifts, I encourage you to look within yourself to reveal your own hidden potential. Each of us has intuition and the capability to use it to our advantage.

One of the reasons it was so important for me to include this chapter goes back to when I was first beginning to explore my gifts. With so much information out there, my longing for knowledge made it difficult to decipher fact from fiction. Furthermore, it is an unfortunate truth that this area of metaphysics is heavily polluted with frauds. That being said, it is my intention to provide you the most accurate and honest information to assist your spiritual growth and journey. You are also being provided a variety of exercises to develop your own psychic gifts.

Before I learned how to hone my psychic abilities, I hadn't had much exposure to the metaphysical world beyond what I read in books or saw in the movies. Initially, I just assumed that a psychic was someone who could gaze into a crystal ball and see your future. Little did I know that many of the thoughts and emotions I experienced (but couldn't explain) on a daily basis were psychic qualities. After an immense amount of introspection, I knew there was something "different" about me that I needed to further explore. I didn't want to feel like any alien anymore.

While sitting in the aisles of a bookstore one day, I came across a ton of information that helped me to understand all the different ways a person could be psychic. By releasing the stereotypical perceptions I'd developed, I would then begin my journey. As you read through the information I've included, I encourage you to set aside what you know about the psychic world and open your mind. May your journey begin!

Psychic Skills

There are literally dozens of psychic ability classifications - many of which will not be discussed in this chapter. Though I didn't want to exclude anything from this book, spirit guided me in eliminating anything that lacked authenticity. The following list is an outline of the most popular psychic skillsets I was guided to include.

Clairvoyance: *Psychics who are clairvoyant have the ability to see things in their mind's eye from the past (retrocognition), present and future (precognition). A clairvoyant who gets their knowledge from a sense of feeling possesses the gift of clairsentience. A clairvoyant who receives messages through audio impressions possesses the gift of clairaudience (not to be confused with speaking with the dead).*

Empathic: *Having the ability to tune into the emotional impressions of a person, place, or animal is called empathy. Empathic psychics are typically sensitive to feelings of pain and distress and often experience the emotions of the person, place or animal they are reading. While some empathic psychics consciously tune into your emotions, others unwillingly experience the emotions of those around them (which may cause feelings of anxiety when in public or surrounded by large crowds).*

Medical Intuitive: *A psychic who can diagnose disease and illness by reading a person's aura or through anatomic visualization. A medical intuitive may also be able to heal the area of the body that's suffering.*

Mediumship: *The ability to communicate with the other side (those who are deceased or in spirit form). While some people classify themselves as a "psychic-medium", it's important to note that not all mediums are psychic (clairvoyant) and not all psychics have mediumship abilities. A real psychic-medium is someone who can speak with spiritual entities as well as see into the past, present, or future.*

Psychometry: *Psychics who possess the skill of psychometry are able to gain intuitive impressions on an object's history by simply touching it.*

Telepathy: *Someone who is telepathic is able to communicate thoughts or emotions from mind to mind. This is most frequently reported as occurring between siblings, twins and best friends.*

Psychic Practices

While not all psychics rely on additional tools or practices, you may find some of the following helpful when developing your gifts:

Automatic Writing: *Messages from the spirit world can be produced through writing (often in an altered state of consciousness). Automatic writing can also help the writer access their subconscious or intuition. On some occasions, automatic writing can be done with paint or by creating drawings through artistic channeling.*

Channeling: *Generally, when a psychic channels, they become a medium for spirits or the divine to communicate through speaking, writing or thoughts. Channeling can also be used to interpret animal thoughts.*

Palmistry: *By reading the impressions on a person's palm, noting hand size or recognizing different shapes, it is believed the reader can see personality traits, past events and insight to the person's future.*

Remote Viewing: *The psychic is able to see distant locations or objects with their mind. Remote viewing is commonly confused with Astral Projection. The difference between the two is: Astral projection requires leaving the physical body to see places/things. Remote Viewing allows the psychic to see with their mind while remaining in their body.*

Scrying: *By gazing into the reflections of a crystal ball, mirror or water (generally while in low light), the gazer is shown different images and messages.*

Tarot Cards: *A deck of cards with symbols or images that each have their own meaning. The questioner shuffles the deck and then spreads out several of the cards. The meaning behind each card is a response to the questioner. A common misconception is that Tarot cards predict the questioner's fate when in fact it's only an imprint of the questioner's future at the present time. Tarot Cards can also be used to gain insight into past and current situations (as well as their influences).*

Tasseography: *The practice of reading tea leaf patterns left in a cup. It is believed the symbols of the tea leaves are created from the energetic imprint left behind by the person who was drinking.*

Detecting Psychic Frauds

If you're looking to get a psychic reading, it's important to know how to distinguish whether or not you're dealing with a charlatan. Keeping in mind that each psychic operates differently and has different skillsets, it is not my intention to discredit someone who possess any of these qualities. The following are simply a few common warning signs to keep an eye out for.

Hot Reading: *By eavesdropping beforehand or in requiring a lot of personal information in advance, this technique allows the reader to generate foreknowledge of their client. Unless you're doing a reading that involves numerology, you shouldn't have to provide your birth date or full name. If you're doing a reading that requires those thing, supply them on the spot (at the time of the reading) to guarantee authenticity.*

Cold Reading: *By considering your appearance and mannerisms, this technique helps the reader to gain insight into their client. By observing body language, the reader is also able to see what you do and do not connect with.*

Leading: *A psychic who asks a lot of questions may be manipulating you. Unless the reader is attempting to validate a message's accuracy or how it applies to your life, stray away from giving details that will lead them to reach conclusions about your situation.*

Vague: *If something seems too general, ask your psychic to further explain the message. While some things can be difficult for a psychic to interpret (they might not know how it relates to your life), stating "you've experienced something difficult in the past" is vague and likely applicable to anyone. Was this "something bad" money, relationship, career or family related? An open (but trustworthy) statement might be: I'm shown in the last year you experienced a significant physical trauma. Even though this could be a variety of things, you now have a timeline and the overall nature of the event (trauma to your body).*

Upselling: *While services do cost money, establish a concrete amount you're comfortable spending beforehand. If you're enjoying your session and want to extend it for an additional cost, that's okay. Just make sure you're not being pressured/scared into spending unnecessarily.*

Getting a Reading

Now that we've discussed how to detect a potential charlatan, the next step is learning how to get the most out of a reading. Below, you will find a few tips to consider.

1. Prepare some questions beforehand. Even though you might go with the intention to discuss one thing and receive messages about another, it's also important you don't walk away feeling like none of your concerns were addressed. It's very easy to lose track of time when a psychic presents something unexpected, but you don't want to end with even more questions than you started with.

2. If you're consulting a medium, it's okay to ask the deceased to validate their presence, but don't be too specific with your expectations. I once gave a reading where spirit kept showing me a college sweater. I had no idea what this meant as it wasn't a symbol that I'd ever used. I asked my client the significance of the college sweater to which she replied there was none. At the end of my session, the client expressed she was disappointed I didn't validate the one thing she wanted to hear from her sister. Apparently, she was fighting with her sister's husband over a lost wedding ring. Two days later, I received a call from my client – her brother-in-law found the ring in the front pocket of her sister's college sweater. Her sister was in fact validating the dispute, but in a different regard than she'd expected.

3. The future is not set in stone. If you're looking for insight about your "fate", remember that most psychics are shown what your future looks like at the current time. If you don't like something, change it! You are the writer of how your story ends.

4. Don't let one bad reading generalize your attitude towards psychics. If you had a negative experience with your doctor (for example), you wouldn't give up on medicine and say it's all lies. I hope that you would instead look for a different doctor who better understands your needs. Psychics are no different! It's not always a reflection of a reader's abilities either – sometimes you just need to find a psychic that you connect with better!

Psychic Exercises

Whether you're a skilled psychic already or just beginning to explore your gifts, it's important to exercise your abilities. Even though it's unlikely you could ever "lose your intuition", challenging your mind to remain active is an important part in maintaining your psychic health. Well-being aside, it can be a lot of fun just seeing what you're capable of! Until you push the limits of what you know, don't rule out your hidden potential.

Test #1 : Grab a notebook and pen. Close your eyes and imagine picking up next week's newspaper. As you try to visualize the different headlines, imagine what it feels like holding the paper, where you're sitting, what you smell, etc. What headlines do you see? Is there a name that stands out in the obituaries? What about sport scores? Once you're ready, open your eyes and write down as many of the details as you remember. In one week, grab the newspaper and see if you were able to correctly predict any of the stories! As you lean where you went wrong, you'll be able to refocus that energy to securing more accurate details in the future. Continue this exercise over several weeks and don't be discouraged if it takes you time to achieve positive results. Track your progress. How specific can you get?

Test #2 : As you shuffle a deck of playing cards, predict the color of the first card that will be dealt. Once you've made your prediction, deal a card face up to see if you were right. Next, shuffle the cards and visualize the specific suit. Again, deal the card and see if you were right. Lastly, try to guess the number of the next card you will deal and see if you were right. Do not think of this as a guessing game. Instead, if you get a card wrong, identify what you misinterpreted from your intuition and try again. This technique should be used to "fine tune" your predictive abilities. Get familiar with identifying the difference between what your mind tells you and what your intuition tells you.

Test #3 : Have you ever received a phone call and known who it was before you answered? Throughout the day, don't look at your Caller ID. Attempt to focus on the energy of who is calling before you answer. Do not think logistically who is most likely to call, as it will defeat the purpose of the exercise.

Test #4 : For this exercise, have a friend draw a simple image on one piece of paper and don't peek! You can either sit back to back or facing, but a few chair lengths apart. As they draw, try to replicate the picture to the best of your ability. When you're done, compare sketches to see the shapes and elements you correctly interpreted.

Test #5 : Find a few small items around the house that you're very familiar with. Place each object into a separate paper bag, fold the tops and shuffle them so you don't know which bag has which piece. Placing your hands above each bag, focus your energy and try to read the energy. See if you can determine which objects are in which bags!

Test #6 : Have a friend hide something around the house and use your mind's eye and intuition to find where your object was hidden. You can also consult your guides to ask for help finding it!

Test #7 : Using 5 notecards, replicate the images seen below (Zener Cards). Have a friend shuffle the cards and focus on them one at a time. As he/she focuses on the image, try to tune into their thoughts and write down which card you believe they're holding. When you're ready for the next image, have them place the notecard face down and repeat with the next card (the goal in mind, to keep them in order). Once you've gone through all of the notecards, flip over the pile to compare with your notes and see if you matched the order correctly!

Test #8: On a day where you're scheduled to see a friend, take some time to meditate beforehand. Visualize what you see them wearing and doing. Write as many details down as possible. When you meet up later, look at their clothes and ask what they did for the day. If you were right, show them your notes and see if they can validate the other details!

Chapter Eighteen

A method used to clear negative spirits & purify people or places.

SMUDGING / CLEANSING

Skill level : Easy
Estimated Time: 5-10 min

Tools

- White Sage
- Abalone Shell
- Match, candle or lighter
- Feather *(optional)*

Directions

5. Slightly open your windows or doors if desired (for air circulation).

6. Light your sage stick with a match, candle or lighter. Once the sage has a flame, gently blow it out so that the tip still smokes from what appears like coals.

7. Hold your sage stick over the abalone shell to prevent any burning particles or ash from falling. Take a moment to focus your energy or say a brief prayer. Ask the universe to clear any negative energy or spirits.

8. Using your hand or a feather, gently wave to disperse the smoke in front of you. If you're cleansing a house, cover all rooms. If you're cleansing a person, gently wave the smoke around their body. Afterwards, they may also cup their hands with the smoke and motion over their head (as if you were rinsing your face).

9. Spaces like stairways, corners, and closets have a tendency to accumulate energy. You may want to spend a little extra time cleansing those areas.

Origins of Smudging with Sage

Smudging is an ancient tradition that goes back thousands of years. While people all over the world have used smoke and incense to drive off insects, evil spirits and to prevent disease, sage is traditionally associated with North American Indian culture. The smoke was believed to carry the negativity and illness into the heavens.

Note from the author

While cleansing, I not only ask that negativity be banished, but that the house or person I'm cleansing be shielded with protective white light. I prefer to smudge until my sage bundle fully extinguishes, though this is not necessary. I also occasionally use white sage with sweet grass which is believed to attract positive energy.

NOTES

Chapter Nineteen

Tarot cards are a useful tool for gaining insight into the areas of your life.

TAROT

Generally composed of 78 cards, the Tarot is a popular psychic tool that dates back to the early 1400's. Initially introduced as a game, people later discovered that Tarot cards could be used for divinatory purposes. Each card is designed with a different picture that's believed to symbolize a message of ancient wisdom. When dealt, the cards are designed to provide insight to the inquirer. The cards themselves can be broken down into two predominant categories:

Major Arcana

Each of these 22 cards reflect pivotal events in your life – they are the universal aspects that make up the human experience. When appearing in a reading, these cards carry a significantly heavier amount of weight than those of the Minor Arcana. When laid out in order, the cards tell the Fool's journey through life; the milestones of our development towards achieving fulfillment. Even though each of us chooses to take a different walk in life, the milestones of the Major Arcana can be applied to everyone.

Minor Arcana

The 56 cards in the Minor Arcana represent the situations we encounter on a daily basis. From the people we meet to the emotions we feel, Minor Arcana represent the influences and little details that affect our journey. The Minor Arcana are divided into four suits that reflect the overall themes of the situations we encounter. Like a standard deck of playing cards, each suit is made up of 10 cards (numbered 1 to 10) plus 4 Court Cards (King, Queen, Knight and Page). The Court Cards represent other people in our life and the aspects of our own personality. Court Cards also reflect the overall qualities of the suit they're found in.

Tarot Spreads

While there's no specific way to deal tarot cards, there are a few spreads that people commonly use. If you're looking for quick insight regarding a situation, drawing a single card may be adequate. In my experience however, at least three cards provides a clearer perspective.

Personally, there are two main arrangements I find myself using. After I've dealt the cards, I always keep the remaining stack readily available. Along the way, if I have any questions about a specific card in my spread, I pull additional cards (one at a time) off the top of my deck to establish a deeper understanding. If my cards say that someone was a negative influence in my life (for example), I might be inclined to pull an additional card in order to gain insight into who that person is. The two spreads I commonly use are as follows:

Quick Reading

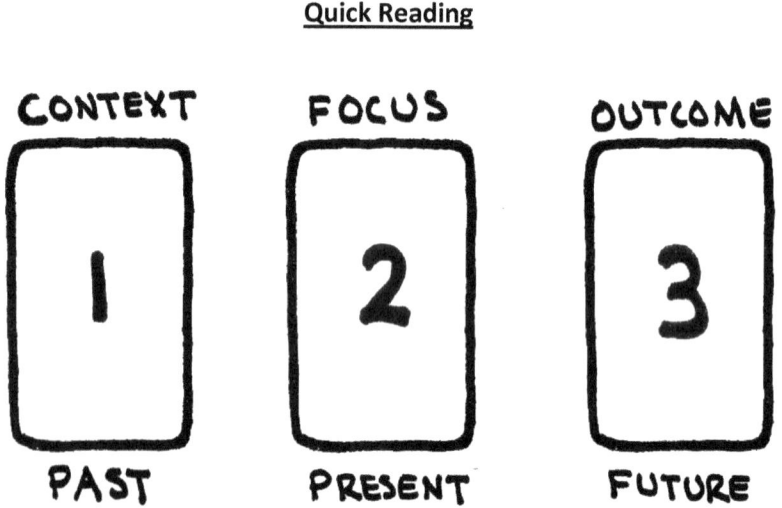

This option requires only three cards and gives quick insight into a person or situation. I find this most useful when I don't have a lot of questions and just want to see the overall picture. If I've drawn the spread for myself, I use the first and second card as a way to validate that the Tarot is in tune with my energy. I won't even consider the third card (outcome) if the first and second cards are out of alignment with my actual past and present. If that happens, simply shuffle and re-draw.

THE DIVINITY DOCTRINE

Traditional 10 Card Spread

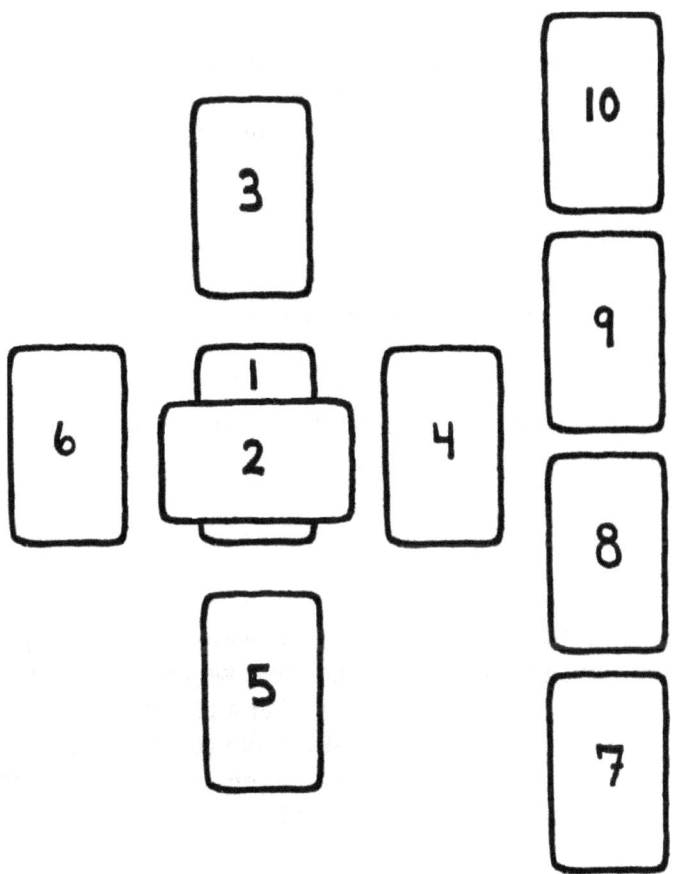

1. **Present:** *What the questioner is currently experiencing*
2. **Immediate Influence:** *Nature of the influence/obstacles just ahead*
3. **Best Outcome:** *The best result that can be accomplished at this time*
4. **Distant Past:** *Major events/influences from past that affect present*
5. **Recent Past Events:** *Recent events that have influenced present*
6. **Future Influence:** *What influence is coming in the near future*
7. **Internal Factors:** *Factors/inner feelings affecting the situation*
8. **Environmental Factors:** *The things that will affect the outcome of the questioner. These things are beyond the questioners control.*
9. **Inner Emotions:** *Hidden hopes, emotions, desires, fears & anxieties*
10. **Future:** *The tentative end result from everything put together if questioner continues on the same path. Can be changed with change.*

Tarot Spreads *(continued)*

Whichever spread you decide to use, it's important to note that the future card is never your "fate" – it resembles the future outcome as it currently stands. If you see something that you don't like, you can make adjustments in your life to attain a different outcome. Also, don't forget that if you're having trouble connecting with a card, you can always draw another card for additional details (after you've completely placed out your spread).

If you're relatively new to Tarot and can't remember what the different layouts mean, it may be helpful to replicate the spreads (and their meanings) on a poster-board. If you don't like the two options in this book, you can always develop your own arrangement or look online for alternative ideas!

Dealing Tarot

Over the years, I've seen a huge divide between readers who prefer the questioner deals their own cards and those who prefer no one touches their deck. Some people even require that a prayer be said before the cards are drawn. The truth is, no matter what you do (as long as you are consistent), the Tarot will know your intentions. Build a relationship with your deck and do what is most comfortable for you!

Depending on who you talk to, the way in which you deal the Tarot also has a significant influence over a cards meaning. By dealing a card vertically, it puts the cards upside down (reverse). Furthermore, some people believe the cards should always be dealt facing the person you're reading. Personally, I no longer acknowledge reverse cards unless I see an overwhelming number of them in a spread – in which case, I re-center my energy and start the spread over. That being said, I also never have to worry about who the cards are facing because it has no influence over whether or not a card is reversed. As this is a general guide, the card descriptions I'm including in this chapter do not include reverse meanings.

** If a card ever falls out while shuffling or dealing, try to acknowledge it separately from the reading as it often contains a helpful message. **

Asking Questions

The most common reason that people consult a Tarot deck is because they're facing some type of challenge or need insight on a situation. While the Tarot doesn't tell a questioner their future, a spread can help with understanding why something is happening and what can be done to ensure/prevent the current outcome. For this, knowing how to ask a question is one of the most important aspects of learning how to properly utilize the Tarot.

The first step is to thoroughly consider everything pertaining to the question. Consider who is involved (directly or indirectly) and what your options are for the future. When you're doing this, don't rule out any possibilities. Many times, we can't even begin to imagine the real way things are going to unfold. Tarot helps to see alternate approaches to a situation. Release any methodical thinking when you're evaluating the full/bigger picture and allow your intuition to lead your thoughts. While you're evaluating your situation, it helps to determine if you have a specific question or if you're simply looking for general insight.

Keeping in mind that the Tarot cards will not make a decision for you, vocalize what it is that you're seeking guidance on. While there are methods to answer "yes or no" questions, it's recommended your inquiry allows more room for the variables you haven't considered. Some examples of good questions are:

- Can you give me insight into...?
- Help me to understand David's intentions.
- What are the influences affecting...?

Be specific with your questions and remember to remain neutral. Make sure that your existing perception isn't influencing the reading. Whenever you assume that the problem is outside of yourself, you rule out the opportunity to change your own thoughts and behaviors that could be affecting things.

Lastly, remember that what you want and what you need may not always be the same thing. If you're in litigation (for example) and ask if you'll get a favorable outcome, understand that by not winning, it might actually help get you to a better place than you even imagined possible.

Major Arcana Meanings

The following list is my interpretation of meanings for the Major Arcana cards. If you've asked a question that doesn't match well with the descriptions provided, consider the card title for face value (and how it applies to your life) or look at the card's art to find your own meaning.

0. The Fool: *As the first card of the Major Arcana, The Fool represents new beginnings and the starting of a journey (spiritual, emotional, career, etc.) or possible travel. You're ready for change and new ideas. Overall, this is a card of energy and fresh starts, though it can also reflect naivety. Be wise with important decisions that need to be made.*

1. The Magician: *Even though you may not see it, you have everything that you need to get what you desire. Like a magician, sometimes it just requires a little sleight of hand and creativity to learn how to use things to your advantage. This card also represents that the lines between the spiritual and physical world are blurred (becoming one within the other). Follow your intuition and put your ideas into motion so that they can begin to manifest.*

2. The High Priestess: *The answers are there (and available), you just have to look for them. Trust your intuition and look within yourself. Be patient and don't push too hard – allow things to happen on their own. This is a card of duality, mystery and hidden influences. The High Priestess also represents the feminine side of the male personality and the influence of women.*

3. The Empress: *A card of maternal and nurturing energy (or a need for it). You may also be treating work and projects like your baby. Depending on the cards it's surrounded by, The Empress can also be a card of creativity, unconditional love, working to bring things to fruition and pregnancy.*

4. The Emperor: *Represents Authority and how to use it responsibly. This card signifies you or someone else in a position of leadership. The overall attitude of this card is reflects laws, structure, order, solving conflict through power and ambition that will bring the possibility of long term success. Achievement.*

5. The Hierophant: *The meaning of this card is dependent on your views. To some, The Hierophant represents a religious figure or authority that provides constructive support; a person of morality and experience. To others, it represents feeling suppressed by too much structure and old systems. Either way, you might also be struggling to find the truth (or come to terms with it). This is a card of routine, authority and guidance.*

6. The Lovers: *The obvious meaning would be a new relationship (or relationship interest). The lovers also represent union and finding harmony as opposites unite. There may also be a struggle to make a decision or commitment about something/someone. Your heart and mind may be battling each other.*

7. The Chariot: *Intentions are manifesting into action. The Chariot represents taking things head on and moving towards a goal (to achieve something good). If you've been struggling, you'll soon be rewarded with success and perseverance. The Chariot itself could also be taken in a more literal sense – a vehicle for travel.*

8. Strength: *Though this card could represent physical endurance, it's more about inner strength and courage. Doing the right thing and being strong-willed when you're challenged with temptation (the easy way out). Be generous and put differences aside.*

9. The Hermit: *The Hermit can represent someone who provides guidance or looking for someone who does. More so, this is a card of solitude, planning and needing to look inward. Doing the right thing is rarely easy and can be lonely, but there's still light.*

10. Wheel of Fortune: *Things come in cycles and are always moving. Things will unexpectedly begin coming to fruition and positive change (and prosperity) is coming. Though it's not always permanent, this is a generally positive card and reminds us that life has its up's and down's.*

11. Justice: *The result will be a reflection of that which is fair. Many times favorable, the choice is most often straightforward. Conflicts are reaching resolution. The Justice card also resembles anything with legal issues, contracts, settlements, marriage, divorce, clarity, equality and judgment (conclusion).*

12. The Hanged Man: *Things are stagnant or feel monotonous. This card can represent self-sacrifice and suffering for a reason (the bigger picture). Even though things aren't "good" or "bad", they seem more like they just "are". Surrendering to the experience. A waiting period and allowing for rebirth / transformation. Feeling overwhelmed.*

13. Death: *Symbolic of slow transition and transformation, this card is more often about letting go of the past than it is about physical death. This can also be about releasing your old self and bad habits. The things that no longer serve a purpose are coming to an end.*

14. Temperance: *Finding a middle ground. Unity of opposing forces to create something (often greater). Things are/will be handled well and come together. This is all about cooperation and successful negotiation.*

15. The Devil: *You are your worst enemy or are dealing with negative influence from others. Feeling trapped and burdened. This card can also represent things such as addiction, pride, lust, corruption, materialism and someone who is only thinking about themselves (being selfish).*

16. The Tower: *Sudden, drastic and unexpected change. Negative and false things are torn down as reality is revealed. Destruction of ego, conflict, and dramatic shifts. Even though it's uncomfortable, it's happening for a reason – you come out stronger and smarter in the end.*

17. The Star: *Spiritual enlightenment and inspiration. Remember that there's light at the end of the tunnel and that life's possibilities are endless. Look to the future and allow your horizons to broaden. This is a card of hope and renewal.*

18. The Moon: *Heavy amounts of uncertainty. The inability to see things clearly due to Illusion, secrecy, mystery, chaos, hidden truths, suspicion and the subconscious. Face fears and explore the unknown to reveal the truth. Also a card that signifies artistic endeavors, psychic abilities and work in the entertainment industry.*

19. The Sun: *A card of happiness in all forms. Shedding truth and defeating disarray. Conclusion after hardship. Spiritual awakening. Returning to your natural state of being. Achieving wholeness, good health and a positive future. Playfulness or child-like energy.*

20. Judgment: *An in important pending decision could change your life for the better. Leaving the past behind to embrace a new beginning that is free from suffering. Legal decisions about a situation have been (or will be) reached. Generally, this card offers a satisfactory outcome and a commitment to correcting wrongdoings.*

21. The World: *This is the last card of the Major Arcana. It represents completion (the end of a cycle, project or phase of your life) and a greater awareness. Everything happens for a reason. Remember that the journey is never over – as one chapter ends, another begins!*

Minor Arcana Meanings

All of the Minor Arcana can be divided into 4 categories. Though the symbols themselves may differ between decks, the meanings generally remain consistent. When conducting a reading, look for reoccurring symbols (theme) to see what the questioners main focus is. A person who has a lot of pentacles (for example) may be concerned with work.

> **Wands:** Wands generally deal with creativity, communication, action and matters of self-improvement/spiritual growth. They are most often associated with situations surrounding confidence, adventure (risk-taking) and things you're passionate about.

I *(Ace of Wands)* – *Spiritual beginnings and divine inspiration. There is a new spark that fuels your desire to pursue something; intense sexual energy, new endeavors, creative expression and passion for all that brings excitement. This is a card that says "go for it".*

II *(2)* – *The ideas you have are fueling you. You must begin finding a logical way to turn them into reality because the time is right to make your move! The power is in your hands but it's time to push yourself beyond your normal limits, take a chance and put things into motion.*

III *(3)* – *You've laid the groundwork and are now just waiting for things to come to fruition. Keep optimistic and see the bigger picture – the things you're waiting for are just ahead! Embrace the change and try to adopt a more long-term perspective.*

IV *(4)* – *You're now able to enjoy the positive results of your hard work. The things you dreamed about can now be experienced in reality and shared/enjoyed with the community around you.*

V *(5)* – *Conflict with career or work. Friendly fighting; competition – an opportunity to grow and prove yourself. Be alert and ready to defend what's yours. If your ideas are being challenged, take advice to improve.*

VI *(6)* – *Victory. You've earned the admiration of others. May signify reward for your efforts and an opportunity to become a leader. The 6 (being that it follows the 5 of wands) can signify that you've conquered your competition. This is a card of achievement. Good news is coming.*

VII (7) – Fighting to stand up for what you believe in. Usually depicted with an advantage over those he is fighting, the character has the upper hand. If there are negotiations, it is a card that you will succeed, but you must make a strong effort to overcome the challenge. Enemies are unable to fully reach you.

VIII (8) – *As a whole, this card represents that unexpected information or action is coming. It's all about setting your sights high and achieving them. The momentum is gaining and speeding to an end. May also be an indication of giving your energy to a variety of projects at the same time. Take careful note to the cards surrounding this card as it may indicate the speed of those events. This is the end to a delay.*

IX (9) – *You're at a crucial moment. While you're near completion, you're in the eye of the storm. It's possible that you are/will be faced with last minute setbacks and challenges. Being so close to finishing, it's important that you know you have the tools you need (even if it feels like you're fighting a losing battle). This is the last test before you can achieve the ultimate success. Stay strong and wait for the right moment.*

X (10) – *You have a lot of weight to carry. It's possible that others are relying too heavily on you or that you've taken on too much to handle. In the end however, you're at the last step before completion and are ready to receive the rewards of your hard work and effort. If you're trying to accomplish a lot at the same time, it might just take longer.*

Page of Wands – *A messenger bringing you opportunities and good news. This card encourages you to be creative which will help you succeed; consider more inventive ideas as solutions to problems because the answers you seek may be in a different direction you haven't considered yet. If you're going to do something, do it wholeheartedly. Get excited about life. The Page of Wands can also represent someone you already know who is about to enter your life. This is a friend you can trust that has your best interest at heart. Their intentions are sincere.*

Knight of Wands – *Traditionally, this signifies travel, progress and new ideas. Overall this card carries energy and courage, though some people may misinterpret the Knight as being cocky and unpredictable. There is a lot of action and not enough thought. Tackle challenges head on, but try to consider all options first. Look for unexpected changes around you.*

Queen of Wands – *The Queen is a strong leader and is focused on what she wants. Though she's independent and self-sustaining, she's also very much an extrovert and enjoys being the center of attention. The queen is a natural born leader and inspires others – she's often very likeable. If you do not connect with these personality traits, it's a message for you to be more bold and courageous with your actions. Share your ideas with others. Believe in yourself and make sure to be direct with others. With wands representing communication, confidence and spirituality, the Queen has successfully achieved an understanding of these traits and encourages you to see those aspects within yourself or the situation.*

King of Wands – *Decisive and passionate. The King represents infinite possibility and having a will (that cannot be broken) to achieve the things desired. While he is the pinnacle of achievement, this can come with feeling self-righteous, a quick temper and a need to be the center of attention. In a reading this card can also represent an authority figure or financial gain. If associated with a specific person, they are trustworthy.*

> **Cups:** Cups deal heavily with inner-emotions and things that affect them (such as relationships and the subconscious). Most of the time, the art on these cards is easily interpreted as they blatantly convey feelings of love, happiness, boredom, depression and loneliness.

I *(Ace of Cups)* – *This card represents emotional and spiritual fulfillment. The opportunity is there, but you must choose to welcome it into your life. This may be a lesson in finding a balance between giving and receiving; many times we're great with one but need help with the other. There's enough abundance for everyone to go around. Being an Ace, this card is a symbol of new beginnings in regards to its suit – things of an emotional nature. This could indicate a new relationship or rekindling a broken one (romantic or otherwise). Be open to possibility.*

II *(2)* – *The two of cups is representative of balance, harmony and mutual respect. Whether romantic or platonic, both of the parties involved feel strongly connected and have similar intentions. Typically, the two of cups is associated with relationships the same way "The Lovers" card is seen in the Major Arcana. On some occasions, this can represent marriage or a commitment between two individuals. To take full advantage of this opportunity, both parties must first appreciate the beauty within their own lives before they can see it within each other.*

III *(3)* – *People coming together with a common goal in mind; there is a sense of community and creative opportunities. This card reminds us to live in the moment, enjoy social events (indulge a little) and to celebrate all that life has to offer. Appreciate the people you have in your life.*

IV *(4)* – *The four of cups is about looking within yourself. Attachments to the past (or boredom) may be preventing you from embracing new opportunities or leave you feeling like you've been dealt a bad hand. There are gifts for you to receive, but your focus is in the wrong place which is preventing you from embracing new/better things. Re-evaluate.*

V *(5)* – *There is a lack of fulfillment and feelings of loss and despair. It's important to know that suffering happens for a reason and that the pain is temporary. Things may not have turned out as you'd hoped, but don't forget to consider what you've gained or still have. This situation will soon pass and be water under the bridge.*

VI (6) – Back to the basics. Find simplicity in life and get in touch with your inner child. Take joy in the small things. This card also represents generosity and kindness (or a need to find those things).

VII (7) – There is trouble distinguishing the difference between daydreams and reality. This can also reflect the potential of one's imagination. Some options or situations may be illusions – everything is not as it seems. Be careful of wishful thinking and the choices you face. The dreamer is able to see the beauty and excitement in all things, but needs to remain grounded (practical) with their efforts and intentions. This card also means that you're being faced with uncertainty.

VIII (8) – You may be feeling emotionally exhausted. This is a time to ask what can be done to establish deeper meaning in life. You're leaving something behind (letting go of the past and things in the present that are no longer beneficial to you). There's been a change in perspective that has you focusing more on your personal truth and less on material possessions. You desire something more meaningful. Though this card may represent feeling disappointed and walking away, it's also the beginning of a new chapter.

IX (9) – The nine of cups represents personal integrity and completion (or being in the final stages in getting there). This is a card of good luck and prosperity. Enjoy the fruits of your labor. There are many options available for you to indulge in (sensual desires, luxury, money, food, etc). Count your blessings.

X (10) – Emotional fulfillment. Relationships and family situations are at peace and harmony. Wishes really do come true (happy endings). Your hard work has paid off and you're now ready to receive all that is great.

Page *of* Cups – Signifies the beginning of a creative project or venture. There is an opportunity for artistic or spiritual expansion (psychic gifts). The Page of Cups brings positive messages about those we love, pregnancy, engagement, marriage, new relationship, travel, etc.

Knight *of* Cups – A charming figure who uses intuition and emotions during quests of romance and seduction. This is a person ruled by their heart and not their head. The Knight is brings along opportunities and ideas. Intelligent, artistic, charming and a dreamer, but easily bored.

Queen *of Cups* – The Queen of Cups is nurturing and sensitive. She is admired for her honesty and for being genuine. She's pure of heart. Often a people person, the Queen is revered as a mother, wife and leader. Possessing a very strong intuition, the Queen could also be a counselor or psychic (someone sought out for advice). Being so empathic, it is also possible the Queen represents feeling emotionally overwhelmed. This card can also signify temptation and flirtation. The unknown may be drawing you in.

King *of Cups* – The King is a master of expression and is cautious with his emotions. Due to his compassionate nature, the King is often seen as a healer of complex issues and imbalances. This card can represent the dynamic between two people as having a mutual understanding. If you're struggling to achieve this stability, the King is a reminder to create balance for yourself in order to attain emotional fulfillment. In a more literal sense, the King can represent an older male in your life, business or a leader.

> **Swords:** Swords can best be categorized as dealing with decisions and conflict. Many of these cards represent struggle, though it's often as a result of our own thoughts or behaviors. Swords are concerned with justice (and truth).

I *(Ace of Swords)* – *The conception of a new idea or situation. This has the ability to go one of two ways; it's a double edged sword. The truth is revealed through logic and justice. Promises are kept.*

II *(2)* – *It's recommended that you take a moment to meditate and pause before making decisions. Because things constantly evolve, you may not see all the options (or outcomes), but know that you have the tools that you need to get through – you just need to rely more on your inner self when making this choice. Do not act out of vengeance. Make a decision that is balanced, moral and harmonious. You're at a crossroads.*

III *(3)* – *Pain and suffering are necessary to grow. This card represents the ugly truth, pain within yourself or seeing the pain of others. Once the sorrow is felt and fully experienced, closure and redemption can happen.*

IV *(4)* – *Set your worries aside and take a moment to ground yourself. This card represents retreat and peace/stillness within the mind. It is a period of recovery or the need for one (take a break). Sometimes, the best ideas and clarity come when we rest our thoughts. Put down your defenses and take a deep breath.*

V *(5)* – *You may feel like you're in this alone. If people are not being supportive, take what you can and do what needs to be done. It's time you pick up the pieces and move on. This card often illustrates exploiting another's weakness; either you've been duped or are tricking someone.*

VI *(6)* – *This is a card of transition and exploring the mind. Though the change is gradual, we're reminded that it's still movement. The journey has been long and tiring but is nearing an end (solutions approaching). There may be feelings of regret, but everything was necessary to help get you to where you need to be.*

VII *(7)* – *Deception and thoughtless behavior. An individual is being greedy or acting impulsively. This card also represents a hidden agenda, dishonor, betrayal and trickery. Also, evaluate your own intentions.*

VIII (8) – Feelings of oppression or being trapped. While some of the circumstances aren't favorable, you are your worst enemy. Your own thoughts or fears are preventing you from acting as needed. It's likely you or someone around you feels powerless and needs rescuing. This card may also represent bad news.

IX (9) – The suffering and doubt is piling up. There is a lot on your mind. This card represents worry, anxiety, nightmares, guilt and generally feeling overwhelmed. May suggest mental or physical illness, mourning, miscarriage and delay. The overall message is "don't worry so much".

X (10) – Death of the old self or destruction from all the things that are weighing you down. Feelings of defeat and hopelessness. In rare cases, this may represent physical death. We are reminded that hope is just beyond the horizon.

Page *of Swords* – Decisive action and keeping control of the situation. Tactful expression to dissolve confusion. If you're feeling hesitant, "go for it". This is a card of intellectual pursuit and freedom.

Knight *of Swords* – On one hand, this card is associated with action, skill and bravery. On the other however, this card represents action without a cause, war and disrespect for authority. As ideas are carried ahead, the Knight may be too opinionated or come on too strong. While searching out new ideas, don't seek out conflict.

Queen *of Swords* – Communication that is organized and perceptive. Acknowledging and cultivating the ideas of others, but remaining a free-thinker. Thoughts put into action. Can also represent someone who speaks for others (a teacher, politician or coach).

King *of Swords* – Mastering intellect and reason. This could represent an authority figure or someone who is in control. Don't misinterpret being passionate or logical as being abrasive or judgmental; intentions are in the right place. This card may also be referring to a person who relies heavily on old systems / traditional ways of thinking.

> **Pentacles:** Pentacle cards are related to career and material/financial stability. The overall theme of these cards often reflect responsibility and practicality. The foundations we require and deal with in our everyday life. Pentacles are about the physical comfort and security of having material things and the physical discomfort and pain of not having them.

I (Ace of Pentacles) – Symbolic of new beginnings and opportunities that are coming. The seeds have been planted for a new source of money (increased prosperity). You may have to take some action to get these things moving, but they're right in front of you!

II (2) – You may be juggling too many responsibilities or debating between two options. This card shows that someone is responsible and capable of maintaining balance. It is suggested however that you learn to adapt to your situation. Take things as they come – one at a time.

III (3) – Skilled in projects and work. Fully invested in becoming a master at what you do. You've earned the right to showcase your abilities and have the respect of your peers. Work ethic and leadership.

IV (4) – Holding onto material things and hesitant to share (possessive). Someone is clinging to their legacy, inheritance or projects.

V (5) – Feeling totally abandoned. Needing help, but not receiving it. This card may also be symbolic of feeling isolated by a spouse, family or the community. Fighting to survive despite circumstances.

VI (6) – There is an abundance of resources with a balance of giving and receiving. Bartering to fulfill each-other's needs (trading skills, money, emotional support, etc.) and charity. Using what you have to help others achieve peace in their life.

VII (7) – You're waiting for your hard work to pay off. This card often represents a commitment towards work, life and dreams, but slow progress. Waiting for the end result. Possible promotion/relocation.

VIII (8) – Dedication towards perfecting that which you do. This is a card of steady progress with the reward in mind (slow but steady wins the race). Someone who takes pride in their work ethic.

IX (9) – Entrepreneurship (self-employment). Have confidence in your work and enjoy what you've accomplished. Financial stability/success.

X (10) – This card is often a reflection of family or financial matters. Honor the elders in your family and share your prosperity. You can have everything you desire, but what's it worth if you don't have anyone to share it with? This card may also signify a family business/tradition.

Page *of* Pentacles – Generally, the Page of Pentacles represents a young person who is taking on new responsibility, career or education. It is a card of immense potential, awakenings and beginnings. Desire to manifest dreams into reality.

Knight *of* Pentacles – Responsibility and commitment to ensuring things are successful. Someone who is loyal and whom you can rely on. Be careful and patient when making plans. While perusing things, consider a more traditional approach so that you can finish what you started.

Queen *of* Pentacles – You are (or need to be) nurturing yourself and those around you. Pay close attention to diet and be more generous with others. The Queen is a master at providing stability for herself and the family. This is a card of independence in regards to your financial situation (security).

King *of* Pentacles – The King of Pentacles represents abundance and mastery in business. This is a card of wealth, stability and the conclusion of a cycle. The King has good intentions and is concerned with making sure everyone's needs are met. The King teaches us that a well-planned approach to things will lead to success.

NOTES

… THE DIVINITY DOCTRINE

STEVEN BINKO : THE PSYCHIC PRINCE
Copyright 2014

TO MY KNIGHTS...

As I sit down to type this final "chapter", I'm overwhelmed with such a feeling of accomplishment. Looking back, I'll never forget the first time that I announced I was developing this book. Though I was only in the beginning stages, there was an overwhelming amount of support. It was because of all of you that I was motivated to push forward and turn my concept into reality.

Even though spirituality has always played a significant role in my life, it wasn't until 2010 that I was truly comfortable with coming public about my gifts. Initially, I was terrified how everyone would respond. For the majority of my life, the only people who knew were my family. Many of you had come to know me for my involvement with entertainment, and I couldn't help but feel that my authenticity would be in question. With the help of my Facebook page and web-series however, people finally had a chance to see what I was all about.

Along the way, there have obviously been people who've done nothing but "rain on my parade". To the haters, I'm grateful that you have also been part of this experience. With each person that challenged who I am, and what it is that I do, I learned how to become more comfortable in my own skin. I'm more resilient now than I've ever been.

I can't say that this has been an easy ride, but to those of you who have fought by my side (my Knights), I'm eternally grateful. You have no idea what it means to me to have the kind of support that I do. I know it's kind of cliché to say "it's because of you that I'm able to do what I love", but it's true! Without each of you, I wouldn't have had the courage to leave my job (as a server) and embrace my life's calling.

Lastly, thank you for including me as part of YOUR journey. I hope that you enjoy (and find useful) what I've put together. I can't wait to get started on my next book!

- Steven Binko

STEVEN BINKO

DEDICATION
(IN NO PARTICULAR ORDER)

My Husband Miguel
Thank you for supporting me in everything that I do. I know that I haven't always made things easy, but you've been there for me every step of the way. You make me feel like I can accomplish anything that I put my mind to. By allowing me to pursue the things that I'm passionate about, you've managed to transform my attitude into one of hope; each day I wake up, I can't wait to see what's ahead. Even if I lost everything I have, just knowing I have you is enough to keep me going. Lastly, thank you for sharing this spiritual journey with me and for listening to me ramble about this book at all hours of the night. It means so much to have a spouse who makes me feel normal when most people would run for the hills. You're an incredible person and I can't say this enough...
I love you infinitely.

Aunt Jeannie
Without you, I don't think I would have had the courage to write this book (or even be public about my gifts). We've been through so much together over the last few years, but somehow you always remind me to smile, see the bigger picture and trust my heart. From the 2am calls to counting clouds (while laying on that pier), it seems we never have enough time. You've been an incredible support and my biggest spiritual influence; we're always learning from each other. Words can't begin to express the level of gratitude, love and respect I have for you.

Marcin Gorski
A lot of people are around when things are good but are nowhere to be found when disaster strikes. As I've watched most of my friends come and go, you've been the one person that's there no matter what. Whether we're taking a stroll through Central Park or thousands of miles apart, you somehow always manage to show me how much you care – no excuses. For that, I thank you. Psychic knowledge aside, there's so many things about the future I'm uncertain about. The one thing I have no doubt about however, is that we're going to be in each other's lives for a long time. I can't wait to see what's ahead!

My Parents & Brother

Dad & Cindy, Mom & Frank and my brother Tyler. Looking at all the things we've gone through (and where we are now), I'm so grateful to have been blessed with you as my family. While most kids only have 1 or 2 guardians to help them pick up the pieces, I've been fortunate enough to have a team of 4 incredibly resilient cheerleaders and a brother to back me up along the way. Each of you have taught me so much about family and fighting for my dreams. I know that I haven't done things the traditional way, but somehow I know that you've each given me the tools I need to achieve whatever I put my mind to. Thank you for loving me unconditionally and for always believing in me.

My Grandparents

Thank you for instilling in me the values that have made me the adult I am today. Furthermore, it means so much to me that you have been as active in my life (and endeavors) as you have. I have so many friends who will never know their grandparents, but I've been privileged enough to build a relationship with each of you. Also, to my Grandma and Grandpa Binko, I want to do a special thank you. The two of you have taken so many risks to help me pursue the things I aspire to achieve. Without the sacrifices you've made, none of this would even be logistically possible. Thank you for making my dreams a reality.

Also, it's important to me that I recognize the following:

Jill Werner, Sylvia Lukowiak, Sammantha Rivera, Jose Masso, Michelle Bissette, Nadeette Torres, Christy Delgado, Jamilia Land, Heather Hawkes, Amy Stenzel, Joey Amato, Madelaine & Ella Maczko, Haley, Alexis & Leslie Richardson, Savanna, Margie & Claude Trull, Greg Klusman, Paul Binko, Jill Starrett, Justin Aaron Morris, JD Perez, Mike McKiness, Ashley Sadler, all of my immediate in-laws (Hector, Ivonne, Joel, Bella, Darlene, Kenny, Judy and Junito), Gregory Henchar, Victor Lopez, Aaron Whittaker, Stephen Whittaker, Tiffany Shave, Mary Riley, Alyssa Pinter, Don Hudson, Dustin Garron, Casper Wright, Matthew Brosseau, Carl Estabrooks, Kalie Sorenson, Yessenia Soto, Charles Williams, Kayla Crews, Anna Bowman, Kim Foust, Joni Mercado, Nick Waggener, Patti Orzel, Brian Davis, Travis Graves, Travis Sanders, Gerald Gutoski, Jason Bingham, Lauren Novak, Alana & Ariel Dookheran, Gabe Givens, Brandon Gray, Mike Guerriero, Jim Littlefield, Dave Fidlin, Jeremy McDonald, Nadine Messenger, Jacob Farmer, Jonathan Namath,

Roxana Parker, Johnathon Rhoades, Michelle Urrutia, Martin Voight, Ethan Wethington, Jordan Miller, Martin Saycon, Breanna Bukowski, Otto Frauenzimmer, Lauren Frackiewicz, Jose Palacios, Lauren Pluto, Dominic Hamilton, Emma Lobo, Gary Roof, Taft Schwartz, Cody Lee, Nicholas Sinthasomphone, Dariana De La Cruz-Rodriguez, Drew Lesser, Marilyn Whitson, Taylor Law, Bethany Ryan, Kelly Byrne, Steven Freay, Olga Radlynska, Alithia Bernatitus, Joshua Kobel, Debs Wandolowski, Allison Kirk, my babies Paige & Raiden, and last but not least, God.

To anyone else that I may have forgotten who has actively been a part of my journey, thank you. I'm grateful for your support.

Special Thanks

Even though I haven't had a chance to meet the following two women, they've both served as a source of inspiration in me pursing this project: Britney Spears and Theresa Caputo. To me, you're both a symbol of strength, and I've enjoyed watching you succeed in doing what you love. If I'm lucky enough to meet you, I would be honored if you'd use the space below to autograph my book.

STEVEN BINKO

CONTACT INFO

The following is a list of places that you can find Psychic Steven Binko online. Keeping in mind that the internet is constantly changing, the contact information below is subject to change.

Website
www.stevenbinko.com

Psychic Facebook Page
www.facebook.com/psychicstevenbinko

General Facebook Page
www.facebook.com/stevenbinkoofficial

LinkedIn
www.linkedin.com/in/stevenbinko

YouTube
www.youtube.com/binko101

Amazon Store
www.amazon.com/shops/stevenbinko

www.ingramcontent.com/pod-product-compliance
Lightning Source LLC
Chambersburg PA
CBHW050638160426
43194CB00010B/1715